YOU ARE AN IP COMPANY

The 12-Step Plan to Increase Your Intellectual Property Influence, Impact, and Income

ALSO BY KARY OBERBRUNNER

The E-Mind
Poetry is the Portal
Blockchain Life
Your Book is Not a Business Card
Show Up Filled Up
Unhackable
Elixir Project
Day Job to Dream Job
The Deeper Path
Your Secret Name
The Fine Line
Called
The Journey Towards Relevance

YOU ARE AN IP COMPANY

The 12-Step Plan to Increase Your Intellectual Property Influence, Impact, and Income

Dr. Kary Oberbrunner
Katherine Rubino, Esq.

ethos
collective

Printed in the United States of America

Published by Igniting Souls
PO Box 43, Powell, OH 43065
www.IgnitingSouls.com

LCCN: 2024912310
Paperback ISBN: 978-1-63680-322-7
Hardcover ISBN: 978-1-63680-323-4
e-book ISBN: 978-1-63680-324-1

Available in paperback, hardcover, e-book, and audiobook.

All Scripture quotations, unless otherwise indicated, are taken from the Holy Bible, New International Version®, NIV®. Copyright © 1973, 1978, 1984 by Biblica, Inc.™ Used by permission of Zondervan. All rights reserved worldwide.

Any Internet addresses (websites, blogs, etc.) and telephone numbers printed in this book are offered as a resource. They are not intended in any way to be or imply an endorsement by Ethos Collective, nor does Ethos Collective vouch for the content of these sites and numbers for the life of this book.

Some names and identifying details have been changed to protect the privacy of individuals.

Third-Party Trademarks: EOS®, Entrepreneurial Operating System®, EOS Implementer®, EOS Implementer Community™, EOS Model®, EOS Process®, EOS Toolbox™, and Traction® are trademarks of EOS Worldwide, LLC, used with permission.

TIFFANY & CO., T&CO., TIFFANY, the color and word mark TIFFANY BLUE, and the design and word mark TIFFANY BLUE BOX, amongst other names and symbols, are trademarks of Tiffany and Company and its affiliates. © 2020 Tiffany and Company. All Rights Reserved.

Instant IP Certification Mark[IP]
The superscript symbol [IP] listed throughout this book is known as the unique certification mark created and owned by Instant IP™. Its use signifies that the corresponding expression (words, phrases, chart, graph, etc.) has been protected by Instant IP™ via smart contract. Instant IP™ is designed with the patented smart contract solution (US Patent: 11,928,748), which creates an immutable time-stamped first layer and fast layer identifying the moment in time an idea is filed on the blockchain. This solution can be used in defending intellectual property protection. Infringing upon the respective intellectual property, i.e., [IP], is subject to and punishable in a court of law.

Legal Disclaimer
The information provided in this book is for informational purposes only and is not intended to and does not constitute legal advice, and no attorney-client relationship is formed. The information and/or documents contained in this book do not constitute legal advice and should never be used without first consulting with an attorney to determine what may be best for your individual needs.

Dedication

Kary's Dedication

To Sarah Grandstaff, my Integrator and President.
You see differently and think differently, and for that, I'm grateful.
Because of you, I have the bandwidth to keep creating IP.

Katie's Dedication

To Keegan Caldwell, Micah Drayton, and Marcus Wolter.
I am grateful for your thought leadership,
encouragement, and friendship.

ACCESS YOUR FREE BONUSES

Enjoy Exclusive Content, Videos, Course, Thinking
Tools, Community/Coaching Opportunities and More

InstantIP.Today/Bonuses

Contents

Part Three: Start

Foreword

By Dan Sullivan

I remember creating my first expression of intellectual property over 30 years ago—a thinking tool I named The Strategy Circle®. It became a foundational piece of what's now known as the Strategic Coach® company and program. Thirty years later, I've created hundreds more thinking tools reflecting an ever-increasing portfolio of patents, trademarks, and copyrights.

The combined monetary value of this intellectual property exceeds several hundred million dollars. Just as significant, our clients have leveraged this intellectual property to create billions of dollars of value in their own companies.

Welcome to the wonderful world of intellectual property.

I've learned that once you start taking your IP seriously, other people will too. And the opposite is true as well. If you don't take your IP seriously, nobody else will either.

Unfortunately, most entrepreneurs don't realize they have IP. Those who do often fail to organize their IP. Most entrepreneurs find out the hard way that you can't optimize your IP until you first organize your IP.

The new world of IP is exciting, and thanks to breakthroughs in technology, it's expanding exponentially. Smart entrepreneurs will create bigger futures by learning how to leverage their IP.

Any new world can also feel intimidating at first. Aside from new terms and tools, you'll also encounter new processes and paradigms. This is why I'm so glad that Kary and Katie, two of my Strategic Coach clients and collaborators, have combined their capabilities to publish this book, a simple plan to help you navigate this new world of IP.

They're both experts in their respective fields. Kary is an IP practitioner and inventor of Instant IP™, a blockchain-based proprietary solution to help protect IP. Katie is an IP professional with years of experience at Caldwell, the fastest-growing IP law firm in America, for many years.

Together, they'll help you gain clarity, competence, and confidence about your own IP. This new awareness will open doors to help you experience greater levels of IP influence, impact, and income.

I look forward to hearing how you apply this new knowledge in your life and business. The opportunities are unlimited, just like the world of IP. The sooner you dive in, the sooner you'll be able to create your own bigger future.

—Dan Sullivan
Co-founder and president of Strategic Coach®,
the world's foremost entrepreneur coach,
and bestselling author of more than 50 books

A Note to You—the Reader

This book comes with the You Are An IP Company Course. It's FREE for you and your team and it's designed to help you increase your IP influence, impact, and income. To access please scan the QR code below and/or visit InstantIP.Today/Bonuses

ACCESS YOUR FREE COURSE

Co-authored books can often feel clunky when two authors keep introducing themselves to readers—who's talking and who's not. Katie and I didn't want to put you through that back-and-forth whiplash. (After all the focus is on you and your IP, not us.) To make the book flow better, most often we write with "one voice"—mine. I distinguish Katie's sole voice when she tells her unique story and shares her IP legal insights. We feel this gives you a better, friction-free, experience. It's more art than science. Enjoy.

Instant IP™

You Are an IP Company™ – Our "Why"

Ideas Change the World

Ideas Are Valuable

People Steal Ideas

Creators Stop Creating Ideas

The World Doesn't Change

Protect Your Ideas Today

Start Changing Your World

PART ONE

STORY

You Are an IP Company That Creates Intellectual Property

If you're willing to explore this statement, then you'll like this book.

But if you're unwilling, you won't.

It's that simple.

A word of warning. If you walk away from this book, you'll also walk away from 90 percent of the value of your company. (The actual number is 96 percent, but we'll land on the conservative side.)

Bottom line: The sooner you see yourself as an IP creator and your business as an IP company, the sooner you'll increase your IP influence, impact, and income.

Be encouraged. It's an incredible time to be alive, especially for growth-minded, abundant, action-taking entrepreneurs. If this defines you—or even if you're open to considering the possibilities—then Katie and I welcome you to the club.

You're among friends.

Your Ideas Are Valuable

Who are you, and what do you do?

It's a question as old as the very first networking event, even if it was a few "cave people" standing around a fire pit, making small talk.

Most people respond with the traditional comments.

> *I am a carpenter, and I frame houses.*
> *I am an entrepreneur, and I build apps.*
> *I am a mechanic, and I fix cars.*
> *I am a beautician, and I style hair.*
> *I am my own boss, and I design video games.*

There are several problems with every response:

1. It's ignorant.
2. It's limited.
3. It's untrue.

These might sound like fighting words, especially at the beginning of a book. But just like we shared a moment ago, you're part of a unique group because you're still reading. As a result, we can tell a lot about you. Namely, you want answers, not entertainment. You want facts, not fantasies.

And for that reason, based on our new world, there's only one true answer to the question: Who am I, and what do I do?

Ready for it?

I Am an IP Company, and I Create Intellectual Property.

The Animation Guy

Recently, I sat next to a man in London. We both attended a workshop. The facilitator, Dan Sullivan, spoke about the power and potential of intellectual property. I turned to the man on a break and asked him if he had any intellectual property.

"No, of course not," he chuckled. "I own an animation studio."

"Really?" I said. "That's fascinating."

"Our clients—LEGO®, Disney®, eBay®, and Google®—they all have intellectual property. But we don't," he explained.

Not wanting to sound combative, I eased into the conversation.

"I'm curious. When you get a new client, do you have a unique onboarding process?"

"Of course," he said. "We have a very clear system we've developed."

"Interesting. And what about when you hire a new employee? Do you have some kind of training that's specific to your company and core values?"

"For sure," he said. "Often, it's why great talent is attracted to work with us."

"Your company sounds amazing. Can I look at your website?" I asked.

I brought up his home page on my mobile device. "I love your logo. Is this IP?"

"Yes," he said.

"What about this phrase, your unique selling proposition? Is that IP?"

"I suppose," he replied.

"You say you animate with, what did you say, *stop motion*? Do you have innovative ways and techniques you've developed? What about pricing plans? Loyalty programs? Company culture initiatives? I'm sure all those big companies don't keep coming back because you're just like every other studio." I pointed out.

"OK, OK. I get it," he said with a smile. "I guess I am an IP Company."

The (IP) Truth Will Set You Free

I wasn't trying to be difficult—quite the opposite. I have a passion to help people publish, protect, and promote their IP. And yet, I meet people every week who convince me they don't have any IP. Then, after about three or four questions or a two-minute visit to their website, they suddenly see themselves and their companies completely differently.

Why do I love helping people protect their intellectual property? Because over a decade ago, my IP was stolen. I know how unsettling it feels, and I never want others to experience what I did. I told that story in my TEDx talk back in November 2023. I didn't know how people would respond to my speech. Based upon the fact that it's been viewed over a million times, I believe other people can relate. Maybe you can too?

I share my story below with the hope that it will help you see yourself and your intellectual property in a brand-new way. If you prefer to watch it, simply scan the QR code below or search on Google "Kary TEDx." (I've come to learn that being a bald guy with a girl's name is at least good for something, in this case, SEO.)[1]

The Intellectual Property Thief (Kary's Quick Story)

In 2010, I did the scariest thing until that point in my life. I published a book about my past struggle with depression and self-harm. At that time, my main job was as a pastor. I had a safe career with salary and benefits. And I was about to reveal my deepest secret. I felt a ton of anxiety because I thought I'd be rejected or perhaps even lose my job.

Instead, something amazing started to happen. My story began helping people around the world who also struggled with the same things I did.

Several months later, I woke up one morning, and unfortunately, through a series of Google alerts, I found out a random guy had stolen my story. He had literally, word-for-word, taken my idea, claimed it as his own, and set himself up as the creator. He had even launched a speaking tour based on the concept. Besides stealing my intellectual property, I felt as though he had stolen a part of me.

What about you? Has anyone ever stolen your idea?

If not, imagine investing your time and money in developing that idea. Long nights. Late meetings. You put everything on the line, maybe even your reputation. You want your idea to help others and solve a problem. Then, without any notice, someone comes in and steals your idea. They kidnap it and sell it again and again, all to make money from the idea that you birthed into the world.

According to the US Patent and Trademark Office, the worldwide sales of counterfeit and pirated goods total between $1.7 and $4.5 trillion annually[2]. Sadly, this crime happens every day. It's a huge problem and not just for those of us who are robbed. We all become victims because stealing intellectual property discourages people from creating new ideas.

I believe ideas are powerful. I believe they can change the world. This is why, one year after I shared my scary story, I took the leap, left my day job, and started down the path of creating a publishing company. It is now my life's mission—igniting souls by setting free world-changing ideas.

And so, over the past decade, I've helped over one thousand authors bring their ideas to life. In my other role, the department chair of entrepreneurship at a university, I help students launch their inventions into the world. I want their ideas to be protected.

Why?

Because ideas are intellectual property, also known as IP, and thus contain value, just like physical property. Think about physical property. We protect and care for it to maintain its value. This is why we put locks on doors and why we mow our lawns. The same is true for intellectual property. We must also exhibit care and protection since ideas are valuable, even more valuable than physical property.

In our parents' and grandparents' days, tangible assets held the most value. This means buildings, land, and supplies. Look no further than the S&P 500 Index, which reflects the value of many of the largest companies in the United States. In 1975, 83 percent of assets were tangible.[3]

But times have changed. In 2020, only 10 percent of the assets were tangible.[4] The other 90 percent were intangible, meaning intellectual property. Take my iPhone®, for example. Ten percent of the value is in the parts and pieces. The other 90 percent of the value is in the IP that makes up the iPhone.

Here's the problem. Traditional ways of protecting ideas—patents, trademarks, copyrights, and trade secrets—take too much time and cost too much money. Imagine being told that to protect your idea with a patent, you must complete an application, pay $30,000, and wait 1–3 years.[5]

After you pay that fee and wait that long, your idea has an 88 percent chance of being rejected.[6] If you want to go a second round and try to protect that idea, you need to pay more money and wait more time. And odds are it will be rejected a second time.

This isn't make-believe. And it's not the storyline for a horror film starring a frustrated inventor. It's the reality for those who want to patent their idea. The bar of protecting your intellectual property is high—way too high.

So, what happens to ideas facing this much friction? Many ideas never see the light of day and end up dying a sad death. We marvel at how many ideas humanity has dreamed up: electricity, medicine, and automobiles. But what about the millions of ideas that never came about because creators couldn't afford the time or resources?

A couple of years ago, I asked a question: What if we could imagine an idea and then—abracadabra—that idea is protected right away, not over multiple years or tens of thousands of dollars?

Well, guess what? That fictional question is now a factual technology. Thanks to blockchain—there's a new way of protecting intellectual property that's much faster, cheaper, and easier than traditional means.

Blockchain is a public, digital ledger. Think of it as a distributed record that everyone can see, but nobody can edit. Blockchain lowers the bar of intellectual property protection so we can all create. The result is a new renaissance of ideas unleashed in every industry—ideas that make our lives easier and our planet better.

We need it because ideas now emerge at a faster pace than ever before. Technology is increasing at an exponential rate thanks to the internet, globalization, and artificial intelligence. According to

Moore's Law, technology doubles every 18 months. And knowledge is exploding. It used to double every thousand years, but today, as stated by IBM®, it's now every 12 hours. This reality has ushered in a new period called the Creator Economy.[7]

I'm not suggesting we need to abolish traditional ways of protecting IP like patents, trademarks, copyrights, and trade secrets. These options might always exist. However, if we want creativity to flourish, we must reduce friction and lower the bar.

The more I explored blockchain, the more I realized it's the perfect solution. It's incredibly secure, but it's also faster and cheaper. And it solves the main issue surrounding intellectual property—timing. In fact, all IP is based upon timing.[8] This is why I could never claim ownership of the golden arches. I didn't protect them in 1962.[9] In fact, I wasn't even around in 1962.

Creating on the blockchain solves the timing question because when you protect your idea on the blockchain, you turn it into a digital asset and simultaneously create a smart contract.[10] That smart contract is time-stamped and immutable, meaning no one can ever change the record of the exact second it was created.[11]

If a bad actor wanted to change the timestamp to falsely claim an earlier date, they'd have to hack 51 percent of the computers in the world and keep hacking it so as to go undetected.

And don't worry about other people taking your idea. You can hide the contents of the smart contract and only produce it in a court of law if you need to prove ownership.

With blockchain-protected IP, we literally open up a brand new world of ideas. With the bar lowered, now everyone can get into the game, play, and create.

Here's a cool story to illustrate the point. In 2006, the American Society of Landscape Architects conducted a study. They asked teachers to take their preschool classes to two different playgrounds in a nearby busy city.[12] The playgrounds were exactly the same except for one thing: the first playground had no fence, while the second playground was surrounded by a fence.

In the first scenario, the children remained huddled around their teacher. They didn't explore or play. Rather, they stayed by her side, afraid to venture out. But the second playground produced different results. Here, the same children played on all the equipment and freely explored all the way up to the edge of the fence.

In a way, we're all still children on the playground of life. Intellectual property protection is the fence that allows us the freedom and safety to keep exploring with our ideas.

It tells others, "Hey, there's a boundary here. You can't just come in and take whatever you want." It gives people an incentive to invent things. Our legal system grants rights to creators since we all benefit from new ideas. Without IP protection, there would be less incentive to invent medicines, products, and brands.

But the height of a fence matters. Too low of a fence, and no one wants to create because their ideas can get stolen. But too high of a fence, and no one wants to create because it costs too much time and money—like patents. Similar to Goldilocks and the Three Bears, we need a solution that's just right…not too high, not too low.

Blockchain is the perfect height and the perfect solution. It provides two important qualities for IP protection: a fast layer and a first layer.

For far too long, the world of IP protection has had too much friction. Anytime an industry is fraught with friction, disruption is not far behind. Look at DoorDash® and Airbnb®. Those companies disrupted the food and hotel industries. We're fast approaching the Uber® breakthrough moment of intellectual property protection, all made possible through blockchain technology.

I'll close with one word I often said on the playground. You probably said it too. Abracadabra. Do you know what it means? It literally means it came to pass as it was spoken, or I create as I speak.[13]

Even from a young age, we knew we were designed to create ideas. We said the word without even knowing its meaning.

Thanks to this new Instant IP protection, we no longer have to hope that the ideas we create are protected. We also no longer have to invest $30,000 dollars or wait 1–3 years.

Instead, we can create as we speak and then protect those ideas immediately.

Welcome to Blockchain: The Future of Intellectual Property Protection.

Abracadabra.

One IP Step at a Time

There's much to unpack in this TEDx about intellectual property:

1. The value of IP and how some people want to steal it
2. Traditional ways of protecting IP
3. A new blockchain-based solution for protecting IP

Katie and I will unpack these three topics in Part 1. You'll get a broad overview of the exciting IP landscape emerging right before our eyes and soon have a deeper understanding of IP than 90 percent of the population. Be encouraged. By the end of this book, you'll be in the top 1 percent.

Knowledge about IP won't change your life or business. However, it's foundational. Our goal is that this knowledge informs you to take action. To help you accomplish this goal, we'll give you a *simple* and *practical* 12-Step Plan.

Each day more and more companies leverage this same plan to increase their IP influence, impact, and income. The infographic below gives you an overview, but in Part 2 we'll take a deep dive into each of 12 Steps.

1 Visualize: CLARIFY HOW IP INCREASES *your* INFLUENCE, *impact* & INCOME.

2 Organize: IP IP IP INVENTORY *your* PAST & PRESENT IP

3 Systematize: ESTABLISH CONTROLS *and* PROCESSES *to* PROTECT YOUR IP.

4 Normalize: INTEGRATE HEALTHY IP HYGIENE *into* EVERYDAY OPERATIONS.

5 Specialize: CHOOSE HOW *to* POSITION *yourself* AND YOUR IP.

6 Verbalize: NAME *and* DESCRIBE YOUR IP TO BUILD DOMINANCE *in your* SPACE.

7 Digitize: LEVERAGE InstantIP™, TURN YOUR IDEAS INTO ASSETS.

8 Monetize: DETERMINE *which* IP SOURCES MAKE *sense* TO YOU.

9 Maximize: IDENTIFY POTENTIAL *Competitors,* CLIENTS & COLLABORATORS.

10 Evangelize: CREATE YOUR COMMUNICATION AND *Marketing* PLAN

11 Globalize: DEVELOP A GROWTH STRATEGY *to* EXPAND IP *impact*

12 Optimize: *Enjoy* IP FREEDOM, FINANCES & FULFILLMENT!

Many teams have framed this infographic and hung it in their board-rooms and offices to serve as a map while navigating their IP journey. Other teams have digested this book in study groups or offsite retreats. Still others have reached out to us personally so we can support their companies in a more focused way. Bottom line, we're here to help. We've included a high res version of this infographic and many other tools including the You Are an IP Company course all absolutely FREE at InstantIP.Today/Bonuses.

Our goal is for you to experience the peace of IP protection so you have the confidence to keep on creating.

I want you to become an IP practitioner, not an IP professional. I'll save the professional role for Katie Rubino. I met her and Keegan Caldwell back in 2022. Caldwell has been the fastest-growing law firm in America for many years in a row.

Back in 2022, I didn't know if Instant IP, my blockchain-based invention, would catch on. I just wanted to help creators protect their ideas in a fast, easy way. Since I was newer to the world of IP, I wasn't sure if I needed a patent. Wanting a professional opinion, I hired the best. Caldwell exceeded my expectations. During the patent process, I saw the power and potential of intellectual property. I wanted to share these findings with all of my entrepreneurial and author friends, knowing it could change their lives and businesses, just like it did mine.

It's similar to the excitement around Bitcoin. (But much bigger and *better* than Bitcoin.) Here's what I mean.

Over the past decade, I've heard so many people tell a similar story:

My friends told me to get Bitcoin back when it was only $_____.
If I would have listened, I'd have $_____ today.

You can hear the regret in their voice. They're disappointed they didn't take action.

Well, if you've ever felt an ounce of regret for not acting on Bitcoin sooner, then you'll feel that only 100x more if you don't act on your intellectual property.

Am I saying intellectual property is even bigger and better than Bitcoin?

I think so, but you be the judge. For starters, there's a big difference between Bitcoin and IP. At the point of this writing, Bitcoin is still a volatile asset. The price goes up and down—on a weekly basis. Intellectual property increases in value. It's predictable and stable.

Katie will share a few statistics that demonstrate this reality, but first, I'll invite her to tell a little about her journey into the world of intellectual property. After reading it, I think you, like me, will gain a deep respect for her credibility in the field.

I'm forever grateful she agreed to co-author this book. I asked her because I wanted you to see the practical side of IP (which I represent) combined with the professional side of IP (which she represents). We believe this combination will give you a unique blend of intellectual property confidence and competence.

Intellectual Property Pays Real Money (Katie's Quick Story)

I entered the world of intellectual property by accident. Growing up, I had no inkling I'd become an attorney, much less an IP attorney. If someone had told me as a teenager that this was my future, I would have responded with laughter and disbelief. The interesting thing about IP attorneys is that most end up in the role by happenstance.

My story began in high school when I applied to college with the hope of becoming a pharmacist. I loved chemistry, biology, and studying drugs, so helping patients seemed like an ideal role for me. During my time at Northeastern, I was fortunate to have the opportunity to spend three semesters on "co-op." During my final co-op, I worked at a compounding pharmacy where I created custom medications for patients allergic to ingredients found in commercial products or in situations where a commercial product didn't exist.

The fast-paced nature and variety of the work kept me excited and motivated. Upon graduation, I took a full-time job at the compounding pharmacy and continued to work there for several years. In 2012, the New England Compounding disaster rocked our world. This left me at a crossroads as to the uncertainty of my professional future. I started researching ways I could expand my career opportunities. That's when I discovered I could apply my pharmacy knowledge and experience to the intersection of the law—through regulatory law, healthcare compliance, and IP. I enrolled in Suffolk Law's evening program and continued to work during the day.

Although I took many interesting classes on various applications of the law, IP intrigued me the most. The concept of protecting assets and driving business transactions through intellectual property sounded fascinating. Upon graduation, I started working with start-ups on their IP strategy, protection, and enforcement. I enjoyed the constant change of pace and laser focus on business outcomes. This mirrored what I loved most about the pharmacy.

I met Keegan Caldwell and Micah Drayton right as Caldwell Law was becoming a fixture within the Boston entrepreneurial ecosystem. Over the next few years, we opened offices in Los Angeles and London and were listed on the INC 5000 list of fastest-growing companies for five consecutive years.

Our approach to IP protection is simple. From the start, we flesh out what clients' business objectives are and then help them obtain and position their IP to achieve it. If clients desire to close a large series A funding round, they need one type of IP strategy. On the other hand, clients who desire to exit in two years will need a different IP strategy.

Over the past few years, we've helped create successful business outcomes for many of our clients. For example, we developed a patent portfolio consisting of 40 different patents that were used to drive an $800 million minority ownership interest in the company. For another client, we built a portfolio of approximately 60 patents that were valued at $300 million and used as collateral for a debt round.

My aim for this book and my work is to educate business owners and entrepreneurs about the value IP can add to their companies. CEOs are often busy juggling competing demands, so unlocking the value of their IP goes unnoticed. IP often plays a critical role in driving successful outcomes, and therefore, it's imperative to learn how to tap into these assets while at the same time protecting them.

How Much Are We Talking?

One of the most common questions I receive from clients centers around the monetary value of their intellectual property. As an intangible asset, the only certain way of assigning a monetary value is to do a formal valuation. However, many entrepreneurs simply want to understand the role IP assets can play in their businesses and if the process makes sense for them. With this in mind, we can arrive at some rough numbers.

Frequently, the sale price of patents sold through business transactions is kept confidential. Until recently, we didn't have good benchmark data on the average value of a patent application. However, in regard to patents sold on the brokered patent market, data is now publicly available.

Think of patent brokers as real estate brokers. They aid in the selling of property assets (patents) and are most frequently utilized when a business is winding up, and some monetary value needs to be unlocked. The key factor to remember is that since this data comes from the brokered patent market where companies are going out of business, these are bottom-of-the-barrel prices. I like to think of these numbers as a benchmark to portray that if a business fails, what is the monetary gain we can expect from these assets we invested in?

In my experience, patents sold through other transactions, such as M&A deals or through enforcement, have a much higher monetary gain, on average.

Average Asking Price of Patent[14]

The data for the values in the table below comes from Richardson Oliver Insights.[15] For the past few years, they have published a report detailing patent values for all patents sold through patent brokers the prior year. The numbers I typically use are the average asking price.

Price per asset	$125K
Price per US issued	$229K
Price per family	$325K

This table demonstrates that as soon as a patent application is filed and on record at the patent office and undergoing examination, you have a business asset with a price tag of approximately $125,000. When the patent application is allowed, the price increases to approximately $229,000. If a patent family is created with a continuation application, the asset jumps to $325,000. We'll take a much deeper look at this process in Step 11-Globalize.

The Average Asking Price of Patent table is only the beginning. In Step 8-Monetize and Step 12-Optimize, we'll unpack many other proven strategies to increase your IP income. Be encouraged; there are dozens and dozens of IP streams of income, not just one.

An Attic Full of Rembrandts

Imagine you're in desperate need of money to pay off family and business debt. Although usually a bad situation, you're in luck. You own some real estate. To make ends meet, you sell one of your properties at a fair market price. You're thrilled about the liquid cash you can now use to pay off the debt—that is, until a story comes out two weeks later.

The reporter reveals that the property you recently sold contained half a dozen Rembrandt paintings. The new owner found them hidden in the attic, wedged between the rafters. Imagine your dismay. If only you had inspected your property prior to the sale, you could have made 100x more money. The new owner isn't about to hand over these newly found assets or any additional income.

This mirrors a story told by Andrew J. Sherman, author of *Harvesting Intangible Assets* and partner at Jones Day. He shared this story in a podcast interview, except he used gold bars instead of Rembrandt paintings.[16]

This situation happens all the time for businesses that sell without taking inventory of their intellectual property. Part of the problem is that IP is often "hidden," just like the paintings in our story (or the gold bars in Andrew's story).

Although not an exhaustive list, here are just a few of the unrealized IP assets "hiding" in plain sight from most entrepreneurs:

1. Brands
2. Processes
3. Relationships
4. Customer loyalty
5. Customer data
6. Logos
7. Employee loyalty
8. Distribution channels
9. Supply chain partners
10. Vendors
11. Best practices
12. Trade secrets
13. Proprietary platforms
14. Copyrights
15. Trademarks
16. Patents
17. Trade Secrets
18. Agreements
19. Products
20. Websites
21. Domain names
22. Marketing funnels
23. Lead magnets
24. Brochures
25. Booklets
26. Webinars
27. Slide decks
28. Publications
29. Royalties
30. Patent applications
31. Certificates of invention
32. Service marks and certification marks, both registered and unregistered
33. Fictional name filings
34. Other source identifiers, such as slogans, vanity telephone numbers
35. Social media handles
36. Software and databases
37. Proprietary know-how, technology or processes
38. Rights of publicity, such as the right to use celebrities' names and likenesses
39. Company know-how
40. Unique processes and methods
41. Slogans
42. Designs
43. New plants
44. Inventions
45. Formulations

And this is just the beginning!

The world of intellectual property gets quite exciting when you start identifying the "treasure" you have in your "attic." After all, you deserve to be compensated for the value you've created.

You'll Know It When You See It

Once your brain is trained to see IP, you'll often see it everywhere. IP is literally found in the straw you drink, the glass you hold, the pen you use, and the hat you wear.

IP takes center stage in the "Cola Wars" between PepsiCo and The Coca-Cola Company, which escalated in the 1970s.[17] IP protection allows brands like John Deere® to build value around its signature green and yellow colors and ultimately win court cases against infringing parties.[18] If you're unfamiliar with the case, here's a snapshot:

> The court found that John Deere's green and yellow color combination has qualified as a "famous" trademark since the late 1960s and that FIMCO intentionally chose the colors to create an association with the John Deere brand. The court also found that FIMCO's use of the colors on its machinery was likely to cause confusion among consumers as to whether its agricultural equipment was made by or endorsed by John Deere.[19]

Can *colors* really be trademarked? You bet. Look no further than Tiffany's. In fact, it's a central part of the Tiffany® marketing strategy and website: Tiffany Blue®.[20] Notice how the jewelry store positions its color:

Tiffany Blue®: A Color So Famous, It's Trademarked

The iconic robin's-egg blue hue known around the world today as Tiffany Blue has been synonymous with the luxury house since the iconic Tiffany Blue Box® debuted. The power of the instantly recognizable color—whether on the Tiffany Blue Box or on jewelry and Home & Accessories designs—cannot be overstated.

While there is no definitive answer as to why Charles Lewis Tiffany chose this distinctive color, some theorize that it was because of the popularity of turquoise in 19th-century jewelry. Turquoise was a favorite of Victorian brides who gave their attendants a dove-shaped brooch of turquoise as a wedding day memento, which increased the color's popularity.

Since 1998, Tiffany Blue® has been registered as a color trademark by Tiffany, and in 2001, it was standardized as a custom color created by Pantone® exclusively for Tiffany and not publicly available. No matter the medium the color is reproduced in, Tiffany's proprietary hue remains consistent and instantly recognizable. The Pantone® color is called "1837 Blue," named after Tiffany's founding year.

An international icon of elegance and sophistication, Tiffany Blue is more than a color; it signifies something greater: it recalls the magic of Tiffany and the assurance that what comes out of a Tiffany Blue Box will always bring joy.

We're just getting started. The world of ideas and intellectual property transcends much more than colors, jewelry, and farm machinery. It's a topic that touches every business and every person, including universities, professors, independent contractors, and employees. IP protection and rights shape the question about who owns a pastor's sermons and books—the pastors who create them or the churches who employ them? This is no small debate either.

Christianity Today discussed this debate in an article over ten years ago titled "Who Owns the Pastor's Sermon?" The editors asked, "Church or pastor? When sermons become books that make millions in royalties, the answer is important."[21]

Fast-forward another decade into the digital economy, and the stakes are higher still. Then again, if you're not used to seeing IP, you'll often miss it. This is why we help our clients "harvest" their IP.

Different professionals leverage different tools to accomplish this task. Katie has a powerful process she leads her clients through in a one-on-one experience. Although we do these sessions with our authors and entrepreneurs, I've also created a simple tool called Instant IP Harvester[IP], which asks five simple questions.

1. Do I have a new way of solving a problem?
2. Do I have a unique idea for accomplishing a task?
3. Do I have a different way of saying something?
4. Do I have an uncommon angle for combining things?
5. Have I created something unlike anything else?

You may find the Instant IP Harvester[IP] tool helpful as you consider your own IP. We've included a blank one as well as a completed version, which I filled out with my own IP and company in mind.

Instant IP Harvester^IP

Question	IP Name	IP Description	Protected
(1) I have a new way of solving a problem.	The Idea Assessment^IP	Your Ideas Are Valuable. It's Time to Protect Them.	Yes via Instant IP ™
(2) I have a unique idea for accomplishing a task.	Book Hook Box^IP	A new way to outline the most important parts of a book	Yes via Instant IP ™
(3) I have a different way of saying something.	Igniting Souls: Unique Selling Proposition^IP	We publish, protect, and promote your intellectual property and turn it into 18 streams of income.	Yes via Instant IP ™
(4) I have an uncommon angle for combining things.	One Sheet^IP	The One Sheet is a tool designed by Kary Oberbrunner to help you clarify your idea before you sell it. When you are intentional and ordered with your thinking on the front end, then you can "market before you manufacture."	Yes via Instant IP ™
(5) I have created something unlike anything else.	The Deeper Path Payoff ^IP	A coaching tool to help clients identify steps they need to take before they realize income.	Yes via Instant IP ™

Before you *optimize* your IP you must first *organize* your IP.
Before you *promote* your IP you must first *protect* your IP.

Instant IP Harvester^{IP}

Question	IP Name	IP Description	Protected
(1) I have a new way of solving a problem.			
(2) I have a unique idea for accomplishing a task.			
(3) I have a different way of saying something.			
(4) I have an uncommon angle for combining things.			
(5) I have created something unlike anything else.			

Before you *optimize* your IP you must first *organize* your IP.
Before you *promote* your IP you must first *protect* your IP.

39

If you want a short coaching video from me on how to complete the IP exercise, please scan the QR Code below or visit the URL. On that web page, you'll also be able to download a fillable electronic version or print copies for your team.

InstantIP.Today/Bonuses

The IP Equation^{IP}

Our goal in writing this book is to help you locate and leverage more of your hidden IP "treasure." It makes more sense when considering The IP Equation^{IP}, built on three important parts:

Your IP + Protect Your IP = IP Value

Let's examine them one at a time.

Equation Part 1: Your IP

By now, you might be curious about all your "gold bars" and "valuable paintings" stashed in different nooks and crannies within your business. If you're like most entrepreneurs, including the animation guy I met in London, you have way more IP than you think.

By exploring the 12-Steps in Part 2, we'll help you identify your IP and then organize it (Step 2-Organize). Even if you're messy or disorganized, our simple tools will help you "declutter" your IP.

Truth #1: You'll never optimize your IP until you first organize your IP^{IP}.

Equation Part 2: IP Value

We'll take a much deeper dive into this topic within Part 2 (specifically Step 8-Monetize). Here, we'll unpack 47 ways to monetize your IP. For now, just remember this concept: *Monetizing Liability for Others*.

We'll down this concept by explaining the Two Purposes of IP:

1. **Security Is the First Purpose of IP**: Intellectual Property protection secures a company's unique inventions and ideas, which is especially imperative for patent protection in the United States, as we are in a first-to-file patent system. Whoever protects their invention first obtains the rights to the invention. Obtaining protection for these unique ideas is necessary before there is public disclosure of an invention, such as at a trade show or launching a product on a website. If you are a sports fan, think about this as going on defense. Defensive strategies involve building a fence that defines the metes and bounds of your land. When considering defense, we identify the strongest ways to protect a company's core technology.

2. **Liability Is the Second Purpose of IP**: Intellectual Property protection creates liability for others, particularly with patents. When competing companies practice an invention protected by your patent, liability is created for the infringing parties. This liability often drives monetary outcomes, including passive revenue streams through a license agreement, driving a judgment through patent enforcement, or being used as leverage to roll up the infringing company in an M&A deal. No matter the outcome, IP value increases when we demonstrate evidence of use by others in the marketplace. Back to the sports analogy, this is considered going on offense. Offensive strategies involve creating barriers and liability for others trying to scale your fence.

Truth #2: When you start taking your IP seriously, other people will too[IP].

Equation Part 3: Protect Your IP

Once you realize you have IP and it contains true value, you're left with a simple choice: Do you protect it or allow anyone to use or abuse it?

Only you can answer this question. But if you had gold bars or Rembrandt paintings, would you leave them in your front yard unguarded, or would you put a fence around your yard?

Naturally, many people wonder how much that fence is going to cost. This is both a wise and fair question. Perhaps you don't have much time or money to invest in constructing a fence. Or maybe your IP isn't fully developed and requires a bigger investment to optimize. Because circumstances are unique, it's important to realize there's no "one fence" that fits all.

Think back to the TEDx fence illustration. Depending upon your goal, sometimes you need a tall, expensive fence like a patent. This will often cost you tens of thousands of dollars and multiple years. But if your IP is worth millions of dollars, then a fence with this type of price tag is an absolute bargain.

Other times, you may simply need a first and fast layer of IP protection like Instant IP. This blockchain-based solution creates a smart contract with an immutable time stamp that verifies the exact second your idea was created. This digital asset can never be changed, and it will be traced back to you as the original inventor. This option is extremely fast and inexpensive. It can even play an important role as "prior art," which invalidates a competitor who tries to patent your invention at a later date.

According to the patent law in the United States, an invention cannot be patented if the claimed invention was…

- Patented or
- Described in a Printed Publication or
- In Public Use or
- On Sale or
- Available to the public

…before the effective filing date of the claimed invention.

With IP, it all comes down to *timing*. This is why we tell our clients: Timing Is Top[IP]. If you're interested in going deeper on the topic of prior art, the USPTO has much to say. We link to several relevant USPTO slide decks accessible here:

InstantIP.Today/Bonuses

As mentioned previously, in the United States, we are in a first-to-file patent system. Timing is also relevant regarding the date you file your patent at the patent office. A good rule of thumb is that the sooner you file a patent application, the sooner you can claim rights in the invention and start creating valuable assets for your growing business.

If you're at the beginning of your IP journey, the variety of IP protection tools might feel complex. If this is you, don't worry. You'll find the IP Protection Comparison Chart[IP] extremely helpful (Step 7-Digitize).

Throughout this book, you'll discover what type of protection you need and at what point in the process. Perhaps you want to use Instant IP first and then move on to a registered copyright, trademark, or patent once you have more clarity about your intellectual property. Obtaining some layer of IP protection will equip and empower you to start promoting your IP, a critical step in monetizing your IP. (More on this in part 2, specifically steps 10, 11, 12.)

Truth #3: Don't promote your IP until you first protect your IP[IP].

Instant IP Circle of Confidence[IP]

Congratulations on completing part 1 (Story). It's time to unpack the steps in part 2. As we said previously, at this point, you already know 90 percent more than the average person when it comes to intellectual property. You should feel an increased level of *confidence* on your journey to increasing your IP influence, impact, and income.

Our coach, Dan Sullivan, has a lot to say about confidence. He believes it's an essential characteristic of all successful entrepreneurs:

> Every entrepreneur's number one responsibility is to protect their personal confidence. When you have confidence as a daily resource, you can learn anything, respond to anything, adjust to anything, and achieve anything. Confidence is the ability to transform fear into focused and relaxed thinking, communication, and action. It's a capability, and when you know how to create that capability for yourself, you can have it in endless supply. This is key to putting your mind into a productive state so you can see the possibilities at hand and create strategies to take advantage of them.[22]

Notice the diagram below. It's made up of 12 steps. Together, these steps form an impenetrable "fence" around your intellectual property, creating a new circle of confidence. This is why we call it the Instant IP Circle of Confidence[IP].

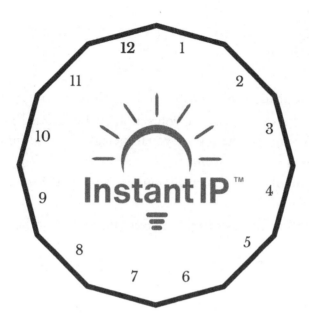

In each of the 12 steps, you'll also meet 12 businesses that see them-selves as IP companies. You've probably heard of some of them. However, up until now, you've probably never thought of them as IP companies.

Similarly, if you want to experience a major breakthrough in your IP influence, impact, and income, you'll need to see yourself differently. Get ready for an identity upgrade.

We don't see things as they are, we see them as we are.
—Anaïs Nin

IP in Five

1. Your ideas are valuable and worth protecting.

2. The sooner you see yourself as an intellectual property company, the sooner you'll increase your IP influence, impact, and income.

3. You'll never optimize your IP until you first organize your IP.

4. When you start taking your IP seriously, other people take you seriously.

5. Don't promote your IP until you first protect your IP.

PART TWO
STEPS

1 Visualize:
CLARIFY HOW IP INCREASES *your* INFLUENCE, *impact* & INCOME.

Taylor Swift® Is an IP Company

Being fearless is having a lot of fears, but you jump anyway.
—Taylor Swift

Many teenagers dream of being pop stars—very few ever trademark their name on the way to becoming one. Taylor Swift is the *exception* and a core reason why she's now *exceptional*.

Swift came to Nashville and signed her first publishing deal with Sony/ATV at the age of fourteen, beginning her professional music career only two years after learning to play the guitar. In 2006, she released her debut album, starting her trajectory to stardom and proving that she had the talent to make it in the music industry.[23]

Wisely, she trademarked her name, "Taylor Swift," in 2007 before she even had a second album. As a teenager, she saw herself as an IP company, not just a singer and songwriter. This move played a major role in ensuring her success in the music industry. At the time of trademarking her name, she had no way of knowing, but her next album, "Fearless," won a Grammy for Album of the Year in

2010. The album included "Love Story" and "You Belong With Me," which are still some of Swift's most popular songs that skyrocketed her popularity in the pop genre.

Since that first trademark, Taylor Swift has proved time and again that she not only has the talent to create music but also the business mindset to protect what she's created. Over the years, she's released 14 albums, four of which, *Fearless*, *1989*, *Folklore*, and *Midnights*, have received Grammys for Album of the Year, something no other artist has done before or since.

Alongside her music, she has filed for over 300 trademark registrations ranging from album titles (including her re-recorded albums), song titles, catchphrases, lyrics (such as "This Sick Beat" and "Look What You Made Me Do"), festivals, tours, and even the names of her two cats, Meredith and Olivia Swift. Owning these trademarks not only solidifies Taylor Swift's brand but also protects it from merchandisers and companies trying to make money off of her work. With each new album and tour, she strategically trademarks important titles and phrases, ensuring her brand is the sole beneficiary.

This isn't the only time Swift has proven she has the business sense to back up her musical ability. Her first six albums were all recorded for the Big Machine record label. After leaving that label in 2018, she started recording with other labels. Big Machine was then purchased, and the albums she recorded were sold to Shamrock Holdings.

In response, Swift re-recorded her albums under Universal Music Group. Swift now owned the masters to these "Taylor's Version" recordings, leading to her re-recording almost all of her albums minus *Taylor Swift* and *Reputation*.

Her gamble of re-recording her earlier albums paid off big time. Swift's staunch protection of her music throughout her career sparked a larger debate about intellectual property in the music industry.

Since then, Swift owns the masters of her later albums, giving her more control over her music and more brand protection.

Taylor Swift embodies a rare musician who has shifted genres while still maintaining her style throughout. Her consistency in lyrics and styles has been matched by her commitment to protecting her intellectual property beyond her music. Through different record labels, recordings, and re-recordings, she's proven her musical and songwriting talent as well as her business savvy for protecting that talent.

But I'm Not Taylor Swift

Maybe you're thinking, "Yeah, but I'm not Taylor Swift. Besides, she's a big star. She should protect her IP."

Firstly, it's a good thing you're not Taylor Swift. (We all agree one is enough.) But secondly, *Taylor Swift doesn't protect her IP because she's a big star. Rather, she's a big star because she protects her IP.* This statement is central to the entire book. It's worth restating again.

Don't protect your IP when you're big. Become big by protecting your IP[IP].

Visualizing is the first step, and Taylor is the first story for a reason. A few years ago, I saw a post going viral on social media. It had two pictures. On the left-hand side, Taylor and a few people, casually dressed, stood with instruments in a park with a lake behind them. On a flimsy makeshift sign, it says Taylor Swift. Only one person—at least by the angle of the photograph—sat on the grass watching.

The other picture of Taylor is quite different. She stands alone on a state-of-the-art stage, dressed in an ornate outfit, sporting tall white boots, surrounded by a packed stadium with tens of thousands of screaming fans. The text on the post says:

Every master was once a beginner. Every pro was once an amateur.
—Robin Sharma

The point is simple. We all start out small. Those who "go big" protect their ideas while they're still small.

As an IP connoisseur, Swift has taken the first step towards adding monetary value to her company. Anybody wishing to promote goods and services relating to "Taylor Swift" has to obtain a license and her permission to be able to do so. This creates another stream of revenue through licensing fees. If someone tries to do so without obtaining her consent, she can legally stop them and be awarded damages. The outcome here is simple: as the owner of a robust trademark portfolio, Taylor Swift has the right to control their use, exclude others, and enforce them for monetary gain.

Should you or your company think any differently about your IP? As Marianne Williamson pointed out, "It's not just in some of us; it's in everyone."[24] Ideas are what makes us unique from any other creature. After all, animals aren't concerned with protecting intellectual property. John Mark Comer tells us why in his book *Live No Lies*:

> One thing that separates humans from the animals is our capacity for imagination. We have the ability to hold unreality in our minds, to imagine what does not yet exist, and then bring it into reality…this is what enables all human creativity.[25]

Bottom line: You were created to create. Whether or not you protect those creations is up to you[IP].

Most Successful Entrepreneurs Miss This

I love entrepreneurs of all kinds. I work with seasoned, successful ones in my companies, and I teach new entrepreneurs at Cedarville University.

When it comes to IP protection, beginner entrepreneurs often out-perform veteran ones. Here's why. Beginners aren't overly familiar with their IP. As a result, their ideas are still novel, and therefore, they feel the need to protect them.

Seasoned entrepreneurs, on the other hand, are overly familiar with their IP. It no longer shines because it's buried in their unique selling proposition or backstage processes. As a result, their IP often goes unnoticed and, therefore, unprotected.

It's important for experienced entrepreneurs to return to square one and visualize what IP will do for them. Anchoring their "Why" makes it easier to protect their "What." This brings us to our first IP exercise we call a "thinking tool."

Step 1 - Visualize: *Clarify how IP will increase your influence, impact, and income.*

Look at the Instant IP Visualizer[IP] below. We've included a blank one as well as a completed version, which I filled out with my own companies in mind.

1. Visualize

Clarify how IP will increase your influence, impact, and income.

	Present IP	**Future IP**
Influence	Leverage TEDx video to build awareness for Instant IP™. Include in company-wide email signatures. Write FORBES articles on Intellectual Property. Updated LinkedIn with TEDx link. Include in Cedarville newsletter and new Instant IP™ website. Chop into reels for social.	Move into a trusted advisor role for key influential centers and leaders. Continue to build currency and credibility within the industry by writing, speaking, and coaching on this topic. Leverage current engagements on social and in person to generate more opportunities.
Impact	Intentional promotion of Igniting Souls and Instant IP™ at key events. Requires travel and face-time with right-fit clients: CoachCon, Abundance, London Blockchain Event, Book-in-a-Weekend with John Maxwell, North Carolina, Cedarville, Lee Brower, PIN, and more. This is the year of strategic collaborations.	Next year we will create collaborative IP. This includes sponsorships, books, podcasts and "Protected by Instant IP™" positioning. Move from being the Product to the Platform. Need to say NO to many "Almost Right Fit" clients. If they want to make the cut, they need to become Seller as we retain Buyer status.
Income	File child patent to keep the door open for new innovation. Turn Instant IP™ Optimizer 12 Step Plan into a new book. Invite strategic co-author. This functions as a lead generator for right-fit clients. Also expands income opportunities as it makes the topic more accessible to growth-minded entrepreneurs and enterprises.	Rather than short-term wins, we play the long game. Consider paypal and *Zero to One* book. Their strategy was to get as many people on the platform. They even paid to do so. Create an Instant IP™ incentive where people can refer someone and each get a credit? The new person (owner level) and the referrer (enterprise level).

Insights	Leverage present IP with strategic marketing. Capitalize face-time in-person events. Stay on look out for right-fit clients and collaborations.	Instant IP™ is a platform not a product. We would benefit from a network effect approach with incentivized referrals and bonuses.
Actions	Write Instant IP™ book to make the topic accessible and spread the idea.	Create Instant™ IP referral program. Say NO to most opportunities

Instant IP VisualizerIP

1. Visualize

Clarify how IP will increase your influence, impact, and income.

	Present IP	**Future IP**
Influence		
Impact		
Income		

Insights		
Actions		

Instant IP Visualizer[IP]

As you complete the IP exercise, it's important to give yourself grace. The goal of these 12 Steps is imperfect action, not perfection. If you want a short coaching video from me on how to complete the IP exercise, please scan the QR Code below or visit the URL. On that web page, you'll also be able to download a fillable electronic version or print copies for your team. If you want to increase your IP influence, impact, and income, it's the doing that matters, not just the knowing.

Remember, the sooner you take your IP seriously, the sooner people take you seriously.

InstantIP.Today/Bonuses

IP in Five

1. Taylor Swift doesn't protect her IP because she's a big star. She's a big star because she protects her IP.

2. You were created to create. Whether or not you protect those creations is up to you.

3. Beginner entrepreneurs aren't overly familiar with their IP. Their ideas are still novel, and therefore, they feel the need to protect them.

4. Experienced entrepreneurs are overly familiar with their IP. It no longer shines because it's buried in their unique selling proposition or backstage processes. Their IP often goes unnoticed and, therefore, unprotected.

5. It's important that we return to square one and visualize what IP will do. Anchoring your "Why" makes it easier when it's time to protect your "What."

2 Organize:

IP IP IP

INVENTORY *your*
PAST & PRESENT IP

Krispy Kreme Doughnuts® Is an IP Company

Our mission is to make the most awesome
doughnuts on the planet every single day.
—Krispy Kreme

For many people, the Great Depression marked the end of their business ventures, but for Vernon Rudolf, it started one of the largest doughnut franchises in history, with over 12,000 locations worldwide.[26]

It began in 1933 when Rudolf's uncle, Ishmael Armstrong, bought the doughnut recipe from a French New Orleans chef. From there, he and his family opened the doughnut business, which ultimately went out of business. Vernon Rudolf, determined to keep the Krispy Kreme brand alive, tried to buy both the name and the doughnut recipe. Unfortunately, he didn't have the funds.[27]

However, his father, who had also been involved in the business, stepped in and bought the company. After a couple of successful years in Nashville, he opened two other shops. Eventually, Rudolf wanted to open his own Krispy Kreme location. He and his two friends headed to Winston-Salem, North Carolina, and spent their last twenty-five dollars renting space on Main Street and setting up the shop. They purchased equipment and ingredients on credit, believing the business would be successful. Rudolf's commitment to quality meant staying true to the original recipe and only selling the best doughnuts.

This wasn't the only distinction that set him apart from the competition though. Rudolf couldn't help but experiment with doughnut-making equipment. He even created a laboratory to standardize automation and ensure uniformity. Krispy Kreme's way of making doughnuts is its true intellectual property.[28]

The demand for Krispy Kreme grew, and Rudolf saw franchising as a way to meet that need. He made it clear that people could own their Krispy Kreme location as long as they agreed to use the secret dough-nut recipe, match his commitment to serving only the highest-quality doughnuts, and maintain consistent branding. With those standards in place, he formed the official Krispy Kreme corporation in 1946. This uniformity in both appearance and actions, regardless of the location, has long been credited with the success of the brand.

Clear IP kept showing up in Krispy Kreme's look, feel, and taste, leading to standardized decor in 1960.[29] Unfortunately, after Vernon Rudolf's death in 1973, the franchise faltered for a couple of years before merging with Beatrice® Companies, Inc. This large corporation executed a different vision than Rudolf's, ultimately abandoning the secret recipe in favor of cheaper costs and higher profits. They even began selling sandwiches, confusing the brand and the customers.

Disregarding the IP proved unwise, and revenue fell, leading them to sell Krispy Kreme. Many early franchisees, led by Joe McAleer, formed a group that bought Krispy Kreme in 1982 and reversed all changes that Beatrice had made.[30] The return to proven IP in terms of what the doughnuts were made of and the process for making them led to its redemption and rise. If you've had a Krispy Kreme donut since 1982, you can thank its IP for keeping the tradition alive.

Even Shark Tank Misses Good Ideas

Krispy Kreme thought its intellectual property resided in the doughnuts themselves, the recipe. In reality, time revealed its most significant IP centered on the way it makes donuts, the process. The truth is, we're not always sure which of our intellectual property will fizzle or sizzle.[IP] A blog post by Emerson Thomson Bennett® explains more:

> Are Krispy Kreme's doughnuts great? Of course! But are they incredibly different from other doughnuts? Not really. Why the secrecy around its recipe? Sometimes, you file something as a trade secret, believing it's important to your success. Then, eventually, you find out that this isn't the case at all, but you never stop keeping the secret because…why tell anyone?[31]

Remember our Rembrandt example about intellectual property hiding in our "attics"?

The problem with Rembrandts is that not everyone knows one when they see one. This is why art critics exist. They can distinguish real from fake.

But this isn't always possible when it comes to the world of ideas. If you've ever watched *Shark Tank*, then you've seen how sometimes the "professionals" pass up multi-million dollar ideas. Other times, they go all in on ideas that never even launch.

In fact, this trend is so frequent that the internet documents the damages. One such article, "Shark Tank: 7 biggest missed investments that went on to make millions,"[32] highlights two of the biggest misses:

1. **Ring** (The smart home security system originally named DoorBot purchased by Amazon in 2018 for over $1 billion.[33])
2. **Kodiak Cakes** (Currently over $200 million in annual sales and sold by large retailers like Whole Foods, Target, and Costco.[34])

Thankfully, these founders didn't let popular opinion kill any of their passion or perseverance. Instead of lying down, they doubled down on protecting their IP. Many times, popular opinions aren't good judges regarding the value of IP.

Rejection and disregard seem to be a common storyline with IP creators of all shapes and sizes, including a very petite one named Lindsey Stirling. The award-winning violinist has scored billions of views on YouTube. Before the world knew her name, she performed on national television on *America's Got Talent*. She was far from award-winning, and the judges let her know. Seconds after her live performance, they delivered their opinions while friends, family, and millions of strangers listened. They said:

> *You've got to be a world-class violinist ... or you'll miss loads of notes...there were times when you sounded like a bunch of rats being strangled.*

> *You're not untalented, but you're not good enough to get away with flying through the air and trying to play the violin at the same time.*

> *You remind me of a little cartoon character. The problem with you is that you need to be in a group. You need a singer. I don't*

think what you are doing right now is enough to fill a theater in Vegas.

Stirling didn't let their opinions dissuade her. Instead, she got down to work and practiced even harder. She also did something else. On January 22, 2013, she protected her intellectual property.[35] She continues to lean on IP protection throughout her career via various copyrights and trademarks.

When It Comes to IP Protection, Don't Delay

I talk to entrepreneurs of all kinds who push off protecting their intellectual property. Their excuses vary, just like their industries. Some don't want to invest the cost of time or money. Others want to wait until the market validates their idea. These entrepreneurs assume delaying doesn't come with a cost. Big mistake! Waiting to protect your intellectual property always comes with a cost.[IP]

Thankfully, the band Twenty One Pilots didn't wait until it blew up before it started protecting its intellectual property.

Although the band literally fills stadiums now, in 2011, Twenty One Pilots traveled to their first show outside their city. Guess how many people came to an unimpressive basement to hear them perform.

Twelve people!

If you watch the clip from that show on YouTube, you'll realize band members Tyler Joseph and Josh Dun didn't hold back.[36] They gave the audience a true performance. And after making it big, they embodied the same enthusiasm playing in front of twelve thousand people as in front of the first twelve.

Years later at the Grammys—the television season's most-watched entertainment telecast—in front of more than twenty million viewers on February 12, 2017, they accepted the Award for the Best Pop Duo/Group Performance with the same enthusiasm.

Here's the secret:

Enthusiasm isn't a result of being on a bigger stage.
Enthusiasm is what gets you on a bigger stage.
Enthusiasm is the cause, not the effect.
It's the root, not the result.

The same is true for intellectual property protection. If you don't take your idea seriously when you have one paying customer, then you won't take it seriously if you have one million paying customers. Perhaps this is why Twenty One Pilots filed their trademark on November 10, 2011, the same year they had twelve people at their concert.[37]

If you ever hope to become a "household name," then you'd better protect that name from the beginning.[IP] The first step in that process is organizing your intellectual property.

Step 2 - Organize: *Inventory your past and present IP.*

Look at the Instant IP Organizer[IP] below. Notice the two columns:

1. Description: What is it?
2. Location: Where is it?

2. Organize

Inventory your past and present IP.

Description (What is it?)	Location (Where is it?)
Clarity attracts. Confusion repels.	In my head.
The Deeper Path Payoff.	A graphic on my computer.
Seek to be valuable, not visible.	In my head.
IP 3 Circles	On my desktop.
Shiny objects are simply dressed up distractions.	In my head.
Success doesn't ruin you. It reveals you.	In my head.
Without loving people there is no leading people.	In my head.
The area of your deepest wound is often the area of your greatest contribution.	In my head.
Soul on Fire 3 Circles	On my desktop.
Selling is serving. Marketing is storytelling.	In my head.

Insights	While writing a book or creating a new project, capture it instantly, the moment I imagine it.
Actions	Protect this IP here on this form with Instant IP™ today.

Instant IP Organizer^{IP}

2. Organize

Inventory your past and present IP.

Description (What is it?)	Location (Where is it?)

Insights	
Actions	

Instant IP Organizer[IP]

Before you can optimize your IP, you must first organize it. Similar to an appraiser who determines the value of something, this appraiser must describe the item and locate it. Both are essential.

There are two attitudes you can choose with this IP exercise:

1. Annoyance for the "effort" it requires.
2. Gratitude for all the treasure you "rediscover."

We've included a blank one as well as a completed version, which I filled out with my own companies in mind. Remember, the goal with this step, as well as the other 11, is imperfect action, not perfection. If you want a short coaching video on how to complete the IP exercise, please scan the QR Code below or visit the URL. On that web page, you'll also be able to download a fillable electronic version or print copies for your team.

As always, the sooner you take your IP seriously, the sooner people take you seriously.

InstantIP.Today/Bonuses

IP in Five

1. We're not always sure which of our intellectual property will fizzle or sizzle.

2. Many times, popular opinions aren't good judges regarding the value of IP.

3. Waiting to protect your intellectual property always comes with a cost.

4. If you don't take your idea seriously when you have one paying customer, then you won't take it seriously if you have one million paying customers

5. If you ever hope to become a "household name," then you'd better protect that name from the beginning.

3 Systematize:

ESTABLISH CONTROLS and PROCESSES to

PROTECT YOUR IP.

Strategic Coach® Is an IP Company

The most valuable property going forward is intellectual property.
—Dan Sullivan

"In July of 1982, I found myself in real trouble," Dan Sullivan recounts the story.[38] "I'd been asked to present writing and artwork for a project I was creating for the federal government in Ottawa. But on the day of the presentation, I had nothing ready to show the cabinet minister.

"I walked down the hall to the meeting where the cabinet minister and four or five members of his team were waiting for me. And I told them that instead of talking about the project, I wondered if I could tell them about an idea I had.

"I addressed the fact that there was an enormous amount of complexity in what the cabinet minister did, and I asked him, 'What are some of the things you want to have accomplished while you're here? What would make you feel great about all of the work you've done?'

"I wrote down his answers and then asked, 'If we were going to prioritize these, what would that look like?' And we arranged the list of accomplishments in order of priority.

"I explained that the next steps were to identify all the obstacles that were currently in the way of those goals and then to work through each one until it was transformed into a strategy for achieving them.

"The minister said this was a fascinating process I had taken him through and asked what I called it. I drew a circle around the goals, obstacles, and strategies and decided then and there to call it 'The Strategy Circle.' He said he wished I'd been there on his first day in office."

My First Expression of Intellectual Property

"I realized as I left that meeting that my whole life, including all the projects and experiments I'd done in the marketplace, had just clicked. I now had a structure that could work for anything.

"The great thing about the structure was that it required no homework on my part. I could simply set up The Strategy Circle, and I would never get trapped like I'd gotten trapped in that presentation situation.

"It wasn't just that I had solved the problem of that particular incident—it seemed that a door to the future had opened for me, and I now had a simple way of approaching the rest of my life.

"I suddenly knew that every time I felt trapped, I could use my imagination to create an immediately bigger framework for taking liberating action.

"Creating a new, bigger game.

"Before that meeting with the cabinet minister, I was coaching, but only in one-off situations. I didn't have a process, and I didn't have a structure.

"In that hour, I felt that I'd done the best work I'd ever done, and it was going in the direction that I really wanted to go in my coaching life.

"The cabinet minister had mentioned that day after, we'd made the list of priorities, that it was easy to get lost in complications and complexity. The Strategy Circle was a way to cut through all of that, and I saw that it could work for anyone in any situation.

"The Strategy Circle was the first thinking tool we patented. At Strategic Coach, we take our intellectual property and protecting that IP very seriously. Although this list needs to be updated on a weekly basis, to date, we've filed 2,000+ copyrights, 200+ trademarks, 42 issued patents, and 65 patents pending.

"Some people ask why. My answer is simple. It's because intellectual property is the most valuable type of property."

The Power of Intellectual Property

Katie and I are both beneficiaries of Dan Sullivan's intellectual property, which he often refers to as thinking tools. As clients, we've experienced the power firsthand and personally. These tools helped me grow myself and my companies. In fact, my Strategic Coach workshops gave me the courage and confidence to create a blockchain solution for protecting intellectual property called Instant IP. It began as a solution for the authors we publish and has expanded to encompass any idea in need of protection created by any entrepreneur.

Those who know Dan Sullivan quickly discover he views intellectual property differently than most. He shares some of these views in a concise video called "What Is Intellectual Property & How To Protect It."[39] I've summarized some relevant points:

> There's a shift going on regarding property. We all know about property in one sense: the land you own or the car you drive. But thanks to the exponential capability of the internet, the most valuable property going forward is intellectual property.
>
> Let's break down these two words. First intellectual. This means you engaged your brain. You looked at a problem, and you discovered a way to solve it. Or you looked at that same problem, and instead of needing eight steps to solve it, you reduced it to three. And the people who use your solution are able to achieve bigger, faster, easier, or cheaper outcomes. This solution came from your brain.
>
> The second word is property. Although you might not be able to see it, touch it, or taste it, the solution you created is property. It's something you now own. In other words, people need your permission to use it. They can't claim it as theirs because it's yours.

Although intellectual property might feel fuzzy when people first learn about it, the concept is solid, even making its way into the United States Constitution. Cornell Law School unpacks the reasons why:

> The Intellectual Property (IP) Clause, also known as the "Patent and Copyright Clause," refers to Article I, Section 8, Clause 8 of the United States Constitution, which grants Congress the enumerated power "To promote the progress of science and useful arts, by securing for limited times to authors and inventors the *exclusive right* to their respective writings and discoveries." It is a foundational document establishing intellectual property rights in the United States, replacing the patchwork of state-law protections that existed in the Articles of Confederation period.

This clause gave Congress the power to enact legislation governing patents and copyrights. For patents, the clause gave Congress the power to grant inventors exclusive rights to their discoveries, allowing inventors to recoup their investment and capitalize on their research.

For copyrights, the clause gave Congress the power to grant authors exclusive rights over their writings. In subsequent federal legislation, such as the US Copyright Act (codified at 17 U.S.C. §§ 101 - 810), the meaning of "writings" has expanded, now encompassing a wide range of artistic and intellectual works, from movies to software.

The utilitarian aim of the Intellectual Property Clause is to maximize scientific and artistic progress. It does so by attempting to balance the incentives it provides for innovation against the chilling effects that limiting access to writings and discoveries may have on novel thought.

Intellectual Property Is a Global Game

Although we take intellectual property seriously in the United States, the rest of the world does too. It's truly a global game. This is why organizations like the World Intellectual Property Organization (WIPO) exist. It's one of the 15 specialized agencies of the United Nations.

Respecting other people's property is a human responsibility and right. Without intellectual property protection, we all suffer. Several sources explain why:

Extracting value from intellectual property and preventing others from deriving value from it is an important responsibility of any company. Although it's an intangible asset, intellectual property can be far more valuable than a company's physical assets. Intellectual property infringement occurs when a third party engages in the unauthorized use of the asset. —Investopedia

Intellectual property (IP) refers to creations of the mind, such as inventions, literary and artistic works, designs and symbols, and names and images used in commerce. —World Intellectual Property Organization

Intellectual property is a broad categorical description for the set of intangible assets owned and legally protected by a company or individual from outside use or implementation without consent. An intangible asset is a non-physical asset that a company or person owns. —Investopedia

Intellectual property rights are the rights given to persons over the creations of their minds. They usually give the creator an exclusive right over the use of his/her creation for a certain period of time. —World Trade Organization

One factor that adds to the fuzziness of intellectual property is the different types of IP protection: copyrights, trademarks, patents, and trade secrets. It's important that your idea receives the right type of protection. "The USPTO grants patents and registers trademarks. The U.S. Copyright Office at the Library of Congress registers copyrights."[40] Here's a breakdown of the four most common types of intellectual property and insight on how to leverage each one:

1. **Copyrights:** Copyrights cover original works fixed in any tangible medium of expression, such as literary, musical, dramatic, artistic, and other intellectual works. Copyrights are granted to authors, whether the original works are published or unpublished. Copyrights protect the books you read, the movies you see, the music you listen to, the software that runs

on your computers and smartphones, and even the blueprints for your home.

IP Insight for Copyrights: Include a copyright notice on works eligible for copyright protection. This typically consists of the © symbol, the year of first publication, and the name of the copyright owner (e.g., © 2024 Jane Doe). If you have obtained Federal Copyright Protection from the U.S. Copyright Office, you can include the federal registration number.

2. **Trademarks:** Trademarks include any word, name, symbol, or design (combination thereof) used to identify and distinguish goods or services and to indicate the source of those goods or services. Trademarks can consist of words, images, colors, sounds, and even smells like the distinctive aroma of Play-Doh®! Trade dress encompasses the visual appearance of your goods or services and packaging. These identifiable marks—and the "look and feel" of your goods—inform consumers that you are the source of these goods.[41] Owners of strong trademarks must be vigilant about protecting their trademarks to avoid losing them if they become generic words such as aspirin, thermos, and escalator.

IP Insight for Trademarks: Use of the ™ symbol can be utilized after a name or phrase that you seek to claim rights in, even if it is not registered. ® symbol: Can be utilized after the United States Patent and Trademark Office grants a trademark registration. It is also recommended to place the ™ or ® symbol on all marketing materials, websites, physical products, and packaging.

3. **Patents**: Patents grant inventors the right to exclude others from making, using, offering for sale, importing, or selling the invention in the United States. There are three types of patents: utility patents, design patents, and plant patents. Patents typically grant a 20-year monopoly.

IP Insights for Patents: Mark products covered and protected by your patents with the issued patent number. If the patent is still pending examination, you can mark the product with the term *"patent pending." If a product is covered by multiple patents and it is too cumbersome to mark the product, you can digitally mark your product by creating a website that lists relevant patent and product information. (More on patent marking in Step 10-Evangelize.)*

4. **Trade Secrets:** Trade secret law provides protection for proprietary information used by a business enterprise. This can include protection for technological and business know-how that is maintained in secret. One of the most famous examples of a trade secret is the exact recipe for Coca-Cola®.

   IP Insight for Trade Secrets: Trade secrets create value by maintaining secrecy surrounding them. The best way to put others on notice about them is to use contractual law through non-disclosure agreements (NDAs) when discussing important details relating to them. Employee education is crucial to those employees exposed to trade secret information. Additionally, ensuring employment agreements contain confidentiality agreements and, potentially, non-compete agreements to shield and safeguard disclosure to competitors, particularly upon employee exit, is imperative.

Brief Overview of IP in the United States

Anthony (Tony) D'Angelo, the founder of The Intellectual Capitalist® and host of *The Intellectual Capitalist*® podcast, explains that IP is one of five asset classes:

1. Paper (Stocks, Bonds, Cash, etc.)
2. Commodities (Gold, Silver, Oil, etc.)
3. Real Estate
4. Businesses
5. Intellectual Property

As we learned in the previous section, IP is the only asset class codified in the US Constitution. According to the United States Court, "The framers of the U.S. Constitution believed that codifying intellectual property (IP) rights at the federal level was important to economic independence, innovation, and domestic growth."[42]

These framers didn't arrive at this conclusion by accident. Rather, they observed a system back in England and integrated it when creating their new country across the ocean. This doesn't mean the system remained static. Instead, over the span of a few hundred years, the focus within IP shifted. D'Angelo explains how in his chart:

The Western Windows of IP History™

Date	IP Focus	Catalysts	Outcome
1700s	Copyrights	Printing Press	In 1710, the Statute of Anne granted authors the exclusive right to copy their works for an initial term of fourteen years.
1800s	Patents	Steam Engine Wealth of Nations Declaration of Independence	In 1790, the Patent Act created the first federal patent office in the US. The first patent was issued July 31, 1790.
1900s	Trademarks	Canals Railroad	On August 30, 1870, the first trademark was registered in the US under the Trademark Act of 1870.
2000s	Domains	Internet	The first domain name registered on the internet was symbolics.com on March 15, 1985.
2020s	Smart Contracts	Blockchain	Time-stamped idea. Frictionless. First layer. Fast layer. Instant IP™. Faster, Cheaper, Easier.

In my recent conversation with Tony, he shared some other points I found noteworthy:

- The location of intellectual property in the Constitution is significant. Since it's in Article 1, it was at the top of the framers' minds and a foundational bedrock of the United States.
- Income from IP is classified as royalty income, as opposed to W2 income. Since this is passive income, it can be offset by other passive losses, such as those from real estate.
- Royalty income is not subject to certain taxes like FICA and Social Security.

Of course, we recommend consulting your CPA for more information on tax savings. However, Tony's point cannot be overlooked. IP is a unique asset class with unique benefits for those who create it and protect it.

New Intellectual Property Class for New Times

Ideas emerge at a faster rate than ever before. Copyrights, trademarks, patents, and trade secrets represent traditional solutions for protecting ideas. They're all valid strategies, and entrepreneurs often use all four in different ways and at different times. That said, these four solutions are often slow and expensive.

New times require new IP solutions.[IP] WIPO understands this and created one back in 2020 called WIPO PROOF. The solution provided a time-stamped digital proof, proving its existence at a specific point in time. PROOF failed to integrate blockchain technology, and WIPO discontinued it on January 31, 2022.[43]

Back in 2021, when I started down my own path to create an IP protection solution rather by accident, I'd never heard of PROOF. As a student of blockchain and a publisher of books, I wanted to create an alternative for intellectual property protection different from copyrights, trademarks, and patents. Since all intellectual property is based on timing, I was hopeful we could produce a "first to use" and "first to file" event via a smart contract created with blockchain technology.

Traditional intellectual property solutions take time and money. At the moment of this writing, a trademark takes on average 12–18 months and a patent 1–3 years. I believe smart contracts could offer an alternative by providing a first layer and a fast layer instantaneously. Everyone could see the exact moment the idea was created, but no one could change the record. The smart contract is immutable, meaning it can never be altered or manipulated.

Thanks to blockchain technology, the new idea is observed via a distributed digital ledger. Or creators could hide the smart contract if they wanted to treat it like a trade secret. This way, no one could see it unless the owner chose to reveal it in a court of law for the purpose of defending it. We called this solution Instant IP because it embodies the very meaning of abracadabra: I create as I speak.

More and more individuals and enterprises now use Instant IP first *before* they move on to traditional means of IP protection. Smart contracts aren't meant to replace copyrights, trademarks, patents, or trade secrets. But thanks to the fast speed and low cost, it's a perfect solution for creators to timestamp when their idea originated. It's frictionless, and available on tablets, computers, and mobile devices. Inventors can go from *Smartphone to Smart Contract*[IP] with the press of a button. Regardless of what type of intellectual property protection vehicle you use, savvy entrepreneurs identify and implement controls and processes that make sense to them. Not having an IP system in place isn't a good strategy, especially because IP is so valuable.[IP]

One of our Instant IP clients, Mark Winters, co-author of the best-selling book *Rocket Fuel,* informed us he established a control to set aside five minutes before he goes to bed each night to record any new ideas he's thought of throughout the day. This way, he can protect the new idea immediately. Rather than letting his new ideas fade, he can now carve them in stone via smart contract. His new idea is time-stamped, proving to the whole world that he thought of it first.

Another one of our clients, Sunny Kaila, founder of IT by Design®, uses a different system to protect his IP. His international company, with five worldwide centers and over six hundred employees, hosts an annual conference. Prior to Sunny taking the stage and delivering content to his clients, vendors, and colleagues, he makes sure to protect his slide deck and handouts via Instant IP. He begins his presentation with a slide and a QR Code that leads back to his smart contracts. We've named it: The IP Speaker Slide[IP]. (View it below and/or download it for use at InstantIP.Today/bonuses.)

> You have my permission to take pictures of my slides. You may have done so without my permission anyways.
>
> **Protected by Instant IP ™**
>
>
>
> Please note, all the Intellectual Property in my presentation is protected by Blockchain Technology using smart contracts. Any usage or reproduction without our written permission is punishable by Law.

Both Mark and Sunny take their intellectual property seriously, evidenced by their controls and processes. As a result, other people take their IP seriously too.

As you clarify your own IP processes, remember three simple steps. We call the process: IP Expert Order[IP]. Get them out of order, and you're in trouble. Keep them in the right order, and you'll stay on the right path:

1. Produce IP
2. Protect IP
3. Promote IP

Step 3 - Systematize: *Establish internal controls and processes to protect your IP.*

Look at the Instant IP Systematizer[IP]. We've included a blank one as well as a completed version, which I filled out with my own IP and company in mind.

3. Systematize

Establish internal controls and processes to protect your IP.

Examples: Backstage, Frontstage, Hiring, Resources, Marketing, Website, Etc.

Control	Incorporate our Protected by Instant IP™ QR Code all public handouts + slides.
Process	Share this commitment at the next Team meeting. Empower "Who's" to execute.

Control	Integrate the Instant IP™ Harvest session for all new Igniting Souls clients.
Process	Include this component in new proposals. Train team on the "How."

Control	Include Instant IP™ Enterprise Ad On with new books. Clients accept or reject.
Process	Share this commitment at the next Team meeting. Empower "Who's" to execute.

Control	Use the new app to protect my own IP when on the fly.
Process	Make sure I have enough Instant IP™ credits in my account. Work with Travis.

Insights	I am not just the creator of Instant IP™, but also a consumer.
Actions	At my next meeting with Travis, share Systematize doc and begin to implement.

Instant IP Systematizer^{IP}

3. Systematize

Establish internal controls and processes to protect your IP.

Examples: Backstage, Frontstage, Hiring, Resources, Marketing, Website, Etc.

Control	
Process	

Control	
Process	

Control	
Process	

Control	
Process	

Insights	
Actions	

Instant IP Systematizer^{IP}

What systems and processes will you start integrating in your IP journey?

Remember, the goal with this step, as well as the other 11, is imperfect action, not perfection. If you want a short coaching video from me on how to complete the IP exercise, please scan the QR Code below or visit the URL. On that web page, you'll also be able to download a fillable electronic version or print copies for your team.

As always, the sooner you start taking your IP seriously, the sooner people will take you seriously.

InstantIP.Today/Bonuses

IP in Five

1. "The most valuable property going forward is intellectual property." —Dan Sullivan

2. The people who use your solution are able to achieve bigger, faster, easier, or cheaper outcomes.

3. New times require new IP solutions.

4. Smart contracts aren't meant to replace copyrights, trademarks, patents, or trade secrets. But thanks to the fast speed and low cost, it's a perfect solution for creators to timestamp when their ideas originated.

5. Not having an IP system in place isn't a good strategy, especially because IP is so valuable.

4 Normalize:

INTEGRATE HEALTHY IP HYGIENE *into* EVERYDAY OPERATIONS.

EOS® Is an IP Company

The Entrepreneurial Operating System® (EOS) is a set
of simple concepts and practical tools used by more than
275,000 + companies around the world to
clarify, simplify, and achieve their vision.
—Mark O'Donnell, Visionary at EOS Worldwide

When we sat down to speak with Mark, we learned much about EOS Worldwide's unique approach regarding its IP.

"Our company founder, Gino Wickman, started his entrepreneurial journey at age 21. After taking over the family business at age 25, he turned the company around and continued running it for another seven years before selling it. During that time, Gino became involved with the Detroit chapter of the Entrepreneurs' Organization and found himself advising many of his fellow EO members. This led to the discovery that he had a passion for helping entrepreneurs and began the vision for what would become the Entrepreneurial Operating System®.

Don Tinney, a business veteran with over 30 years of experience leading entrepreneurial teams and also our company's co-founder, met Gino during the early stages of EOS. After joining forces with Gino and reproducing his results in implementing EOS with his own clients, Don became the second EOS Implementer®. Together, the two of them started to build the EOS Implementer Community™ before officially launching EOS Worldwide in 2008.

At EOS, we've helped thousands of companies break through the ceiling of complexity and get everything they want from their business. Gino created EOS by working with entrepreneurial companies and experimenting with hundreds of tools and concepts before landing on a simple set that created the most significant impact in the least amount of time. He captured those tools in his best-selling book *Traction: Get a Grip on Your Business*. That book has sold millions of copies and is helping entrepreneurs worldwide.

By helping companies implement a complete set of tools, EOS helps leadership teams get better at three things: Vision, Traction, and Healthy.

1. **Vision** is getting everyone in your organization 100 percent on the same page with where you're going and how you plan to get there.
2. **Traction®** instills focused discipline and accountability throughout the company so that everyone executes on that vision every day.
3. **Healthy** is helping your leaders become a more cohesive, functional, healthy leadership team.

We start with the leadership team, getting them 100 percent on the same page with the vision, executing well, and gaining traction while moving forward as a healthy, fun-loving team. As goes the leadership team, so goes the rest of the organization. EOS will help you reach the point where your entire organization, top to bottom, is experiencing vision, traction, and healthy.

EOS consists of three parts:

1. The EOS Model®
2. The EOS Process®
3. The EOS Toolbox™

Several hundred thousand business leaders with 10 to 250 employees have achieved rapid growth and a more balanced life by running on EOS."

Protect Your IP and Give It Away?

If you visit the EOS Worldwide Website, you can download the tools for free. It's the top left button labeled FREE TOOLS.

In fact, EOS encourages you to use them in black and white: "Help your business grow and thrive using the simple, timeless, and practical principles of EOS found in these free tools and eBooks."[44]

But why?

EOS Worldwide takes its IP very seriously. It publishes at eosworldwide.com a comprehensive set of branding guidelines designed to help protect its IP and avoid confusion in the marketplace.[45] With this in mind, why does EOS Worldwide allow anyone to download tools for free?

The business model supports it.

EOS Worldwide allows businesses to use the tools for free because it believes many of these same businesses will then hire an EOS

Implementer® to help them "implement" the operating system. Sure, some organizations will self-implement, but the majority will one day want an outside expert who's been appropriately trained on the tools.

EOS is, therefore, literally an IP Company. Without protecting its tools, other individuals and organizations could come and take their tools and claim them as their own. Simply put, if competitors had bad intent, they could pirate unprotected tools. Logically, this could significantly impact the overall integrity of the business. How? It would cheapen the model and dilute the brand, no longer ensuring purity and clarity.

So, does this IP protection strategy work? Absolutely! And not just for EOS. It's a common practice for many businesses.

Alex Hormozi, author of *$100M Offers* and *$100M Leads*, not only supports this logic, but he teaches it as a proven sales strategy. "Give away the secrets for free and sell the implementation."[46] Or if you don't want to give away your IP for free, then give some of it away via a trial or sample. Most software as a service (SaaS) businesses depend on some form of freemium model for people to get familiar with the product before they buy it. This may include limited use or perhaps a slimmed-down free version. If you want to unlock the full benefits and advanced features, then you have to pay a license fee to use the IP.

There's nothing wrong with sharing your IP, like EOS Worldwide or authors or musicians who give away their work for "free." Authors might share a sample chapter on Amazon. Musicians often upload their songs on YouTube. But this strategy only works if you protect your IP first. For this reason, it's important that creators and companies normalize protecting their IP by integrating healthy IP hygiene into everyday operations.

Step 4 - Normalize: *Integrate healthy IP hygiene into your everyday operations.*

Look at the Instant IP Normalizer[IP]. We've included a blank one as well as a completed version, which I filled out with my own IP and company in mind.

4. Normalize

Integrate healthy IP hygiene into your everyday operations.

		WHO	DO
Step 1:	Change all book QR Codes from Powered by to Protected by	Ethos PM	Done
Step 2:	Ensure my app login has Instant IP™ Credits to protect on the go.	Travis (Tech)	Done
Step 3:	Integrate all slide decks to include customized intro slide with "Protected By" QR Code	Ruthie (Assistant)	Done
Step 4:	You are an IP Company forthcoming book introduces superscript ^{IP} versus ™, ©, ®.	Jill	Done
Step 5:	Include Instant IP™ QR Code on New Client Proposals	Jamie	Done
Step 6:	Purchase branded shirts for all team members	Ruthie	Done
Step 7.	Include Instant IP™ Enterprise line item in all new proposals	Jamie	Done
Step 8:	Include Branded Journal and Pen in all new client packages	Jamie	Done

Insights	Now that the app 1.0 is tested and launched it's time to promote.
Actions	Final meeting with the app team to integrate all updates for 1.0.

Instant IP Normalizer^{IP}

4. Normalize

Integrate healthy IP hygiene into your everyday operations.

		WHO	DO
Step 1:			
Step 2:			

Step 3:			
Step 4:			

Step 5:			
Step 6:			

Step 7.			
Step 8:			

Insights	
Actions	

Instant IP Normalizer[IP]

What steps will you take to integrate IP hygiene? It may feel a little awkward at first, kind of like flossing your teeth for the first time. However, this new "IP hygiene" will pay big dividends and create a culture of health and vitality.

As you complete this thinking tool, we encourage you to also identify what we call your IP Infrastructure[IP]. It's the result of answering three powerful questions:

1. **Team:** *Who's going to own the IP role within your company?* We suggest designating someone to be the Chief IP Officer[IP] (CIPO[IP]). Tony D'Angelo says, "Just like you need someone to manage physical property, you also need someone to manage your intellectual property." Unlike managing physical property, managing intellectual property doesn't need to be difficult.

2. **Tools:** *What's your go-to tool when a new idea is created?* Is it filing a copyright or trademark? Or perhaps Instant IP? We've pre-loaded the app with a FREE smart contract for you to try (InstantIP.app).

3. **Track**: *Where are you going to keep track of your protected IP?* Is it a Google doc or spreadsheet? Our clients use the Instant IP app. This way, they can hide their protected IP or show it off to the world. (InstantIP.Today/protected).

Remember, the goal with this step, as well as the other 11, is imperfect action, not perfection. If you want a short coaching video from me on how to complete the IP exercise, please scan the QR Code below or visit the URL. On that web page, you'll also be able to download a fillable electronic version or print copies for your team.

As always, the sooner you take your IP seriously, the sooner people take you seriously.

InstantIP.Today/Bonuses

IP in Five

1. It's important to normalize protecting your IP by integrating healthy IP hygiene into your everyday operations.

2. IP hygiene may feel a little awkward at first, kind of like flossing your teeth for the first time. However, this new "IP hygiene" will pay big dividends and create a culture of health and vitality.

3. "Give away the secrets for free and sell the implementation." —Alex Hormozi

4. There's nothing wrong with sharing your IP...but this only works after you protect your IP first.

5. "Just like you need someone to manage physical property, you also need someone to manage your intellectual property." —Tony D'Angelo

5 Specialize: CHOOSE HOW to POSITION yourself AND YOUR IP.

CrossFit® Is an IP Company

CrossFit® is a fitness program that produces measurable outcomes
through lifestyle changes centered on training and nutrition.
Workouts consist of constantly varied, high-intensity,
functional movements and are most fun and effective
among friends at a local CrossFit gym.
—CrossFit

Imagine a global brand that makes over $4 billion in revenue centered
around high-intensity fitness training. What's the secret? First and
foremost, it sees itself as an IP Company.

CrossFit, a style of training focused on exercising the whole body
and designed to encourage long-lasting fitness, has managed to
bring in large amounts of revenue through its unique and relentless
trademarking strategies.

CrossFit was created by Greg Glassman, a fitness instructor who
developed the workout strategy while training police officers in the
90s. He began to implement the program in his own gym, eventually

creating the CrossFit brand that made its way to other gyms across the country. Interestingly, the brand doesn't just make money directly from its CrossFit classes and competitions, but also through licensing.

Rather than scaling the business by opening CrossFit gyms across the country, the company allows gyms to purchase licensing rights if they want to use the CrossFit brand. This has allowed CrossFit to grow quickly and profit through independent gyms.

CrossFit has also expanded its trademarks to include apparel, food, and training equipment, ensuring that the brand is protected from infringement. To maintain this protection, CrossFit sends frequent cease and desist letters to those infringing upon its trademarks. The company has also created a specific set of guidelines for how the CrossFit trademark should be used.

The Balancing Act of Branding

Establishing clear guidelines is a smart IP move for CrossFit. It protects the brand from genericide, a situation that occurs when a term becomes so synonymous with its service or product that it ceases to be protected by trademark. A brand is in trouble when the public starts using the trademarked term to identify goods or services in lieu of the trademark being used as an identifier of the source of goods or services.

Once a trademark is deemed generic on the spectrum of distinctiveness, it loses all legal protection as it no longer identifies the source of goods or services associated with it. Some terms that became generic over time include aspirin, bubble wrap, jacuzzi, chapstick, escalator, velcro, lite beer, soft soap, and cola.[47]

Most companies enjoy the thought of global domination. Additional influence, impact, and income aren't bad things. However, when brands rise in popularity without employing IP strategies, they're in danger of genericide. By having specific guidelines and enforcing trademarks, CrossFit is able to maintain its profitable licensing, ensuring it remains a global brand, not a generic term.

According to Cornell Law School, although brands cannot necessarily control how the average consumer uses their trademarked term, they can take certain measures to reduce the chances of genericide.

1. It is important to add descriptive terms beside the products to avoid the brand name becoming genericized, such as "disinfectant wipes" for Clorox.

2. Companies should not refer to their products in a generic way, like using the term as a verb.

3. Companies should take care to use legal channels when someone infringes on a trademark because otherwise, this may exacerbate the genercide process. Also, some companies attempt to use marketing campaigns as a way to change the way consumers refer to their products.[48]

We can reduce the risk of genericide by employing best practices. LegalVision® suggests four:

1. Always use the ® symbol in connection with your trademark. This will increase the chances of consumers recognizing the sign as a brand rather than a generic term.

2. Use your mark in conjunction with a noun. For example, "Buy a Kleenex® tissue" as opposed to "Buy a Kleenex."

3. Never promote your trademark descriptively. For example, Google® does not encourage using the phrase "Google it."

4. Enforce your rights at an early stage. If you become aware of someone using your trademark, take action immediately to stop the conduct and educate and remind the public about the proper use of your trademark.[49]

These days, monitoring your brand is easier than you might think. Several software programs exist, ranging in cost from free to minimal to enterprise. Tools like Google Alerts, BuzzSumo®, and MARQvision™ track, scan, and alert you when your brand is mentioned. These platforms can eradicate counterfeits, unauthorized sales, and infringers across multiple social media channels, the Internet, and publications.

A Tale of Two IP Companies

Both CrossFit and Orangetheory Fitness® are exercise companies, but each has built value and protection around their IP via the application of different business models.

CrossFit operates as an affiliate business model that allows gym owners to become independently licensed affiliates. Each affiliate is an independent owner of his or her business, but they are granted rights to use and promote CrossFit materials and CrossFit intellectual property in conjunction with their own branding. Most often, each affiliate independently owns his or her own intellectual property. Typically, affiliates have more control to run his or her affiliate business as he or she wishes. Affiliates are remunerated for sales, clicks, or leads generated through their co-promotional activities.

Orangetheory, on the other hand, operates as a franchise business. In this model, individuals or groups (the franchisee) are granted the rights to operate a business using the branding, products, and business model of an established company (the franchisor). Franchisees own and operate their specific location or business under the franchisor's brand and system, but they must follow strict guidelines and procedures set by the franchisor.

Franchisees don't own their own IP. Rather, everything is promoted under the name of the franchisor. Many times, customers are unaware of the business model in place as it usually isn't promoted to consumers. For example, businesses such as McDonald's®, ACE Hardware™, and Dunkin' Donuts® all operate as franchises.

Regardless of the business structure, business owners need to have strong agreements in place that clearly define IP usage by affiliates and franchisees. Identification of which IP is being granted to use and which is not is critical, along with uniform guidelines describing how franchisees and affiliates can position branding on marketing materials and websites, is paramount. Brand value is gained through consumer recognition, which ensures uniform usage and consistent marketing materials.

Same Tools Different Tactics

Although CrossFit and Orangetheory Fitness structure themselves differently, both leverage IP and, specifically, trademarks. In fact, trademarks highlight the distinctiveness and the way a company positions itself and the way it specializes within the industry.

Trademark distinctiveness refers to a trademark's ability to identify the source of a particular product or service and distinguish it from those of others. In trademark law, distinctiveness is crucial because it determines whether a mark is eligible for protection. Trademarks can fall into several categories based on their level of distinctiveness:

1. **Fanciful Marks:** These are invented words with no meaning other than as a trademark (e.g., "Kodak®" for cameras).
2. **Arbitrary Marks:** These are common words used in a way that is not related to their ordinary meaning (e.g., "Apple" for computers).

3. **Suggestive Marks:** These marks suggest a quality or characteristic of the goods or services but require some imagination to connect them to the product (e.g., "Netflix®" for a streaming service).

4. **Descriptive Marks:** These directly describe a feature, quality, function, or characteristic of the goods or services. Descriptive marks are not inherently distinctive and can only be protected if they have acquired secondary meaning (e.g., "Holiday Inn®" for hotels).

5. **Generic Terms:** These are common terms for products or services and cannot be protected as trademarks (e.g., "bread" for a bakery).

The more distinctive a mark (fanciful or arbitrary), the stronger and more easily protectable it is. Descriptiveness is considered on a spectrum, with fanciful and arbitrary marks considered the most distinctive and being afforded the highest level of protection. Descriptive marks, on the other hand, must acquire secondary meaning to be protected, and generic terms are never protectable.

Step 5 - *Specialize: Choose how you will position yourself and your IP.*

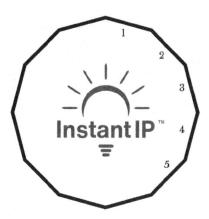

Look at the Instant IP Specializer[IP]. We've included a blank one as well as a completed version, which I filled out with my own IP and company in mind.

3. Systematize

Establish internal controls and processes to protect your IP.

Examples: Backstage, Frontstage, Hiring, Resources, Marketing, Website, Etc.

Control	Incorporate our Protected by Instant IP™ QR Code all public handouts + slides.
Process	Share this commitment at the next Team meeting. Empower "Who's" to execute.

Control	Integrate the Instant IP™ Harvest session for all new Igniting Souls clients.
Process	Include this component in new proposals. Train team on the "How."

Control	Include Instant IP™ Enterprise Ad On with new books. Clients accept or reject.
Process	Share this commitment at the next Team meeting. Empower "Who's" to execute.

Control	Use the new app to protect my own IP when on the fly.
Process	Make sure I have enough Instant IP™ credits in my account. Work with Travis.

Insights	I am not just the creator of Instant IP™, but also a consumer.
Actions	At my next meeting with Travis, share Systematize doc and begin to implement.

Instant IP Systematizer^{IP}

3. Systematize

Establish internal controls and processes to protect your IP.

Examples: Backstage, Frontstage, Hiring, Resources, Marketing, Website, Etc.

Control	
Process	

Control	
Process	

Control	
Process	

Control	
Process	

Insights	
Actions	

Instant IP Systematizer^{IP}

How do you want to position yourself and your IP? Do you want to license your IP? Do you prefer a business model that includes affiliates or franchises? What do you want clients to say about you now or in the future?

Remember, the goal with this step, as well as the other 11, is imperfect action, not perfection. If you want a short coaching video from me on how to complete the IP exercise, please scan the QR Code below or visit the URL. On that web page, you'll also be able to download a fillable electronic version or print copies for your team.

As always, the sooner you take your IP seriously, the sooner people take you seriously.

InstantIP.Today/Bonuses

IP in Five

1. When brands rise in popularity without employing IP strategies, they're in danger of genericide.

2. Companies should not refer to their products in a generic way, like using the term as a verb.

3. Different business models lend towards different ways of leveraging IP.

4. An affiliate program is different from a franchise program.

5. The more distinctive a trademark, the stronger and easier it is to get protection on it.

6 Verbalize:

NAME *and* **DESCRIBE YOUR IP TO BUILD DOMINANCE** *in your* **SPACE.**

MY IP

SEEDSPARK® Is an IP Company

Often, the real game-changers in your
business are the things you're already doing,
but haven't yet named and packaged.
—Chad Jenkins, SEEDSPARK® CEO

"The best way to predict the future is to create it," Chad Jenkins shared with me as he pointed to a framed quote in his office. "This is one of the central art pieces in my office as a steady reminder of the power of innovation. Our team has come a long way since our early days as a Blackberry application development team nearly twenty years ago. Throughout our entire evolution, from applications and managed IT to digital marketing and cybersecurity, our focus has been on our clients and how we can leverage the right technology to help create their future.

"At SEEDSPARK, we are continuously innovating. Weekly, we generate intellectual property because ideas fuel our growth. Some become new product lines or even entire businesses, while others sit, waiting for the right moment to take off. But here's the key: the instant I have an idea, I protect it. That's where Instant IP comes in. Time is precious, and I don't have time for friction.

"Two recent ideas gaining traction at SEEDSPARK are:

1. **Remove the FILM**^{IP}: *Discover Your Business's Potential*

"In the race to innovate, the true treasures are often right in front of us, obscured by the ordinary. At SEEDSPARK, we reveal untapped value within your existing assets. Like peeling the film off a new device, we guide businesses to look beyond the familiar, questioning and connecting the dots to uncover exponential opportunities for growth. Innovation isn't just about the ***new***—it's about seeing the potential in what's already there and elevating it.

2. **Just Add a Zero**^{IP}: *Redefining Success in the Modern Marketplace*

"Where competition once dictated progress, collaboration now paves the way for exponential growth. By shifting from competition to collaboration, businesses can unlock unprecedented potential. I introduced this paradigm shift where collaboration delivers unique solutions, driving both growth and leadership in the marketplace. At SEEDSPARK, we help businesses redefine success by thinking bigger—sometimes, all it takes is to just add a zero.

"Names matter. They create identity and express ownership. Every new idea, every new innovation, needs a name to give it life. Without it, the idea remains stagnant. But when you name it, you breathe life into it, and only then can you share it with your team, your clients, and your Hero Target.

"That's why I created Name the Baby^{IP}—a tool designed to help entrepreneurs and innovators give their ideas an identity, fostering emotional connection and ensuring memorability.

"Naming is about more than just words. It's about defining your IP and differentiating yourself in the market. It's what separates the exceptional from the average."

How the Name the Baby Benefits You:

"Name the Baby inspires entrepreneurs to ignite creativity and think beyond their usual frameworks, offering a competitive advantage for their businesses.

How It Works:

1. **Establish Identity and Ownership:** Give your creations a unique name that solidifies clarity and ownership.
2. **Foster Emotional Connection:** Names create ownership and emotional attachment, making decision-making more instinctual.
3. **Enhance Memorability:** Simplified communication makes your offering stand out, and in a crowded marketplace, that is priceless.

"I've included both a blank and completed version of the Name the Baby tool that we've used successfully at SEEDSPARK. Please scan the QR Code below or visit the link below to download your copy and start naming your next big idea."

InstantIP.Today/Bonuses

Name your IP before you Claim your IP

Chad takes naming IP seriously. We like that. According to the Bible, the first human's job was to name things, animals in fact.[50] Naming is a powerful exercise signifying ownership of that thing. We see this in God's statement to the first humans, "Let us make humans in our image, in our likeness, so that they may rule over the fish in the sea and the birds in the sky, over the livestock and all the wild animals, and over all the creatures that move along the ground."

Even today, we observe how authors name their books, musicians name their songs, artists name their masterpieces, and designers name their products. Think about people who have a pet. What do we call them? Owners. And what do owners do? They name their pets.

Naming something signifies ownership. This is why it's essential you name your intellectual property. Chad's tool—Name the Baby—will help you create a unique name for your idea.

I've known Chad for years, and had the privilege of serving as his book publisher. Chad is a unique man with a unique talent for creating collaborations. He's created over 100 of them, and every single one bears a unique name. Before it gets a name, it's just a thing. But the moment it gets a name, then it has an identity and the ability to be protected. Without a name, you can't protect the intellectual property.

Step 6 - Verbalize: *Name and describe your IP and build dominance in your space.*

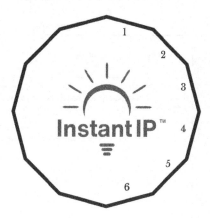

Look at the Instant IP Verbalizer[IP]. We've included a blank one as well as a completed version, which I filled out with my own IP and company in mind. It's fairly simple. You just name and describe each expression of intellectual property.

6. Verbalize

Name and describe your IP and build dominance in your space.

Name	Description
Smartphone to Smart Contract[IP]	A quote by Kary Oberbrunner
One Sheet[IP]	The One Sheet is a tool designed by Kary Oberbrunner to help you clarify your idea before you sell it. When you are intentional and ordered with your thinking on the front end, then you can "market before you manufacture."
Your Secret Name Official Book Trailer	Your Secret Name Official Book Trailer by Kary Oberbrunner
Book Hook Box[IP]	The Book Hook Box[IP] - Kary Oberbrunner
Idea Assessment[IP]	Your Ideas Are Valuable. It's Time to Protect Them.
Igniting Souls: Unique Selling Proposition[IP]	We publish, protect, and promote your intellectual property and turn it into 18 streams of income.
Intellectual Property Circles	IP Publication. IP Protection. IP Promotion.
Clarity attracts. Confusion repels.	A quote by Kary Oberbrunner
Igniting Souls: 18 Streams of Income	The 18 Streams of Income to create a book based business.

Insights	The moment I create an idea is the moment I need to protect the idea. An idea becomes intellectual property the moment it's protected.
Actions	With the new Instant IP™ book I need to protect the ideas prior to presentation and publication.

Instant IP Verbalizer[IP]

6. Verbalize

Name and describe your IP and build dominance in your space.

Name	Description

Insights	
Actions	

Instant IP Verbalizer[IP]

If you feel the process is still a little fuzzy, don't worry. I created another tool named Instant IP Descriptor[IP]. Many clients find it useful because it extracts a name based on the unique benefit produced by the IP.

Instant IP Descriptor[IP] Bring clarity to your creation

	My Example IP	Tips
IP Name	The One Sheet[IP]	*Choose a unique name. First Google it and search USPTO trademarks.*
IP Overview	A tool designed by Kary Oberbrunner to help you clarify your idea before you sell it.	*Who is the creator? What makes it unique? Is it an invention? Original design? A literary or artistic work, statement, or chart? List the date you first started using it.*
IP Benefits and Features	When you are intentional and ordered with your thinking on the front end, then you can "market before you manufacture." This helps you earn influence, impact, and income before you begin.	*What value is created by the IP? What problem does the IP solve?*

	Your IP	Tips
IP Name		*Choose a unique name. First Google it and search USPTO trademarks.*
IP Overview		*Who is the creator? What makes it unique? Is it an invention? Original design? A literary or artistic work, statement, or chart? List the date you first started using it.*
IP Benefits and Features		*What value is created by the IP? What problem does the IP solve?*

122

Remember, the goal with this step, as well as the other 11, is imperfect action, not perfection. If you want a short coaching video from me on how to complete the IP exercise, please scan the QR Code below or visit the URL. On that web page, you'll also be able to download a fillable electronic version or print copies for your team.

As always, the sooner you take your IP seriously, the sooner people take you seriously.

InstantIP.Today/Bonuses

IP in Five

1. "The moment I have the idea is the moment I protect the idea. This is why I love Instant IP. It's simple and easy. I don't have time for fiction, and neither do my companies." —Chad Jenkins

2. "In the quest for innovation, the treasures often lie within reach, obscured by the familiar." —Chad Jenkins

3. "Unless we 'Name the Baby,' our idea will sit lifeless. But once we give it a name, then we breathe life into the idea. Now we can share the idea with our teams and stakeholders." —Chad Jenkins

4. Naming something signifies ownership.

5. Before it gets a name, it's just a thing. But the moment it gets a name, then it has an identity and the ability to be protected. Without a name, you can't protect the intellectual property.

7 Digitize:
LEVERAGE InstantIP,™
TURN YOUR IDEAS INTO ASSETS.

FORTNITE® Is an IP Company

*In many ways, FORTNITE® is like a social network.
People are not just in the game with strangers; they're playing with
friends and using FORTNITE as a foundation to communicate.*
—Tim Sweeney, Founder of Epic Games, Inc.®

Since *FORTNITE*'s release in 2011, the video game has emerged as one of the most popular games in history. However, in the beginning, success wasn't immediate or certain. Epic Games originally created *FORTNITE* to be a sandbox game where players could build and play in order to survive, similar to *Minecraft*®. However, the original concept soon shifted into a battle royale version. Players connected on headsets, and engagement soared, leading to communities popping up all over the world.

FORTNITE wasn't content with the status quo. Instead, the designers kept creating more and more IP via recurring updates. The game constantly adds new features, capturing players' interest. These updates often include seasonal characters, celebrities, and real-life events that correspond with pop culture as a way to keep people interested in the game. This mixed reality experience is defined by the ability to purchase new digital "skins" to adorn your character.

Similar to other examples we've seen in the book, *FORTNITE* fosters a free-to-play system. Rather than making money directly from the game, they designed a free version across multiple platforms with optional upgrades for additional fees. Trademarks play a major role in helping them monetize the game.

Epic Games applied for the *FORTNITE* trademark on December 9, 2011.[51] This was the same year they released a teaser trailer, although *FORTNITE Battle Royale* was released about six years later on September 26, 2017.[52] Between those dates and for many years after, they trademarked other terms from the game, giving them the ability to monetize merchandise. These trademarks help Epic Games collect significant profits and prevent others from merchandising the game. It's just another example of an IP company that utilizes strategies for both offense and defense.

Digital Disruption Is a Good Thing?

I remember when my son got into *FORTNITE* many years ago. It started as an evening activity after school, a way to blow off some steam and connect with his friends. Then, when the pandemic hit, *FORTNITE* became a lifeline for many young people to socialize and maintain healthy relationships during lockdown. While some teens suffered from depression due to isolation, others stayed mentally healthy by engaging in friendly competition online.

On Christmas morning one year, my son opened a gift envelope with a *FORTNITE* gift card. I kept hearing the term V-Bucks, and it finally made sense—kind of. According to *FORTNITE*, "V-Bucks is our in-game currency used to purchase items."[53]

Items? Like physical hats, shirts, and shoes?

Nope. Items like digital outfits, pickaxes, wraps, and emotes!

And what is an emote? (I had to *Google* it too. BTW: That was an intentional example of genericide.) "Emotes are short actions [that] are performed by the player character. Emotes involve the player character acting out one of several actions, such as a Dance, an Emotion, a Greeting, or other movements. Emotes offer no in-game advantage and often disadvantage players with limited movement capabilities."[54]

Did you catch that? Teens are spending literal money in exchange for virtual currency, which can be exchanged for their characters to do a digital dance on the screen.

We might be tempted to judge. Although I've never played *FORTNITE*, I know plenty of adults who purchase digital items for various online games. If those aren't your thing, then like me, you've probably used your smartphones to digitally purchase coffee, air travel upgrades, licenses, tickets, and much more. Digital integration is a necessary strategy for most businesses, churches, organizations, and universities to survive and thrive.

The 6 Ds of Tech Disruption

My friends and futurists Peter Diamandis and Salim Ismail have much to say on the topic of digitization. One of my companies, Igniting Souls®, had the honor of publishing their incredible book, *Exponential Organizations 2.0*. Naturally, we protected their IP via Instant IP as we do with all of our authors.

On the topic of digitization, Diamandis wrote an insightful blog post.[55] Recently, I asked Peter if I could share and summarize his research. Being one of the most generous people I know, he didn't disappoint. His exact words were, "Yes, of course! Anything I can do to support you, my friend." On that note, thank you, Peter, once again, for spreading your ideas (IP) so freely.

The 6 Ds of Tech Disruption are a chain reaction of technological progression, a road map of rapid development that always leads to enormous upheaval and opportunity.[56]

1. Digitization

Anything that becomes digitized enters the same exponential growth we see in computing. Digital information is easy to access, share, and distribute—it can spread at the speed of the internet. Once a product or service can be represented as "1s and 0s"—from biotechnology to music—it becomes an information-based technology and enters exponential growth. Consider the digitization of music leading to new digital products and services, such as streaming platforms like Spotify® and Apple Music®.

2. Deception

Once something is digitized, its initial period of growth is deceptive because exponential trends don't seem to grow fast at first. Doubling 0.1 only gets you 0.2, then 0.4, and so on. At this phase, everything looks like "zero." But exponential growth really takes off after it breaks the whole-number barrier. 2 quickly becomes 32, which then becomes 32,000 before you know it. New digital products and services are often dismissed or underestimated by traditional players in the industry. Consider the classic examples of Blockbuster and Netflix or how Uber and Airbnb went unnoticed by the taxi and hotel industry, respectively. The impact is not immediately apparent, and existing giants don't see what's coming.

3. Disruption

The new market disrupts the existing market for a given product or service that the exponential technology creates because digital technologies outperform in terms of cost and effectiveness. If you can also snap, store, and share photographs, why buy a camera and film? New digital products and services start to gain traction and disrupt the existing industry. This often leads to significant changes in market share and business models as powerhouses struggle to adapt to the new reality. Change or die becomes a reality, not just a slogan. Extinction is inevitable for many leaders who owned the space not long ago.

4. Demonetization

Money is increasingly removed from the equation as technology becomes cheaper—often to the point of being free. Software is less expensive to produce than hardware, and copies are virtually free. You can now download any number of apps on your phone to access terabytes of information and enjoy a multitude of services at costs approaching zero.

5. Dematerialization

Separate physical products are removed from the equation. Technologies that were once bulky or expensive—cameras, GPS, calculators, maps—are now all in a smartphone that fits in your pocket.

6. Democratization

Once something is digitized, more people have access to it. Powerful technologies are no longer only for governments, large organizations, or the wealthy. Entrepreneurship and innovation increase, often creating significant social and economic benefits.

In the Middle of the Digital Revolution

What does digitization have to do with intellectual property? Turns out, these days, everything. As I shared in my TEDx talk, intangible assets currently account for 90 percent of the S&P 500's market value.[57] This is a record high and highlights the value companies place on their IP. This value is juxtaposed to 1975 when intangible assets only made up 17 percent of the S&P 500's market value.[58]

But why the transformative shift? Simply put, digital disruption.

Peter Diamandis's 6Ds are accurate. Many industries find themselves caught somewhere within one of the "Ds." We've experienced the dot-com technology boom of the 1990s and the current data science and artificial intelligence boom we are living in today. We're often told necessity is the mother of invention. Today, that adage couldn't be more accurate.

We've seen massive shifts in company operations in the past few months since the arrival of ChatGPT and other LLMs. We feel the untapped potential in data and technological advancements that once seemed far off or impossible are now our reality. The same is true for our intellectual capital.

Instant IP Is a Simple IP Solution (Katie's story)

When I first met Kary back in 2022, his initial innovative idea as a book publisher was to include QR codes on the back of books that linked back to non-fungible tokens (NFTs). Since these NFTs existed on blockchain, the book can be traced back to the author. Kary wanted to give his authors another level of confidence their ideas could not be stolen.

In two short years, he has transformed his company to solve a bigger problem: How do we timestamp and prove ultimate ownership of the IP we're all busy creating? I see this problem arise almost every day in my law office. Companies are continuously innovating and creating unique processes and inventions that allow them to operate faster. However, they get so busy inventing they forget to take a step back and focus on protection. Sometimes, the problem is even larger. They might not even appreciate the nature of what they have created.

Kary recognized this problem and created a solution, Instant IP. With a quick upload, an idea can be timestamped, capturing the moment of conception and attributing ownership back to the creator. I've seen Instant IP become faster and easier, offering a unique benefit to companies of all shapes and sizes. You don't have to be techy to use Instant IP. With the click of a button, you go from Smartphone to Smart Contract[IP].

As I've helped Kary file multiple patents for Instant IP, we've identified the uniqueness of the invention. For all the fact-finders out there, here's how it works:

Instant IP is a patented, blockchain-based solution for digitizing intellectual property. It utilizes proprietary digital fingerprinting technology to uniquely identify each asset. By employing an immutable smart contract, Instant IP validates the origin of the asset through immutable timestamping and verifies its provenance, effectively proving ownership.

These features play a crucial role in conflict resolution and ensure the authenticity of the IP. The solution is both tamper-proof and transparent. A unique digital fingerprint of the IP is created and stored on the blockchain alongside a timestamp. This fingerprint can be publicly accessed, allowing anyone to independently verify the integrity of the IP. To validate that a file has remained unmodified since its original timestamp, one can generate a new fingerprint from the file and compare it to the one stored on the blockchain. If the fingerprints match exactly, this confirms the document is an authentic copy of the original and has not been altered. If even one character has been changed, the digital fingerprints no longer match.

This system is cryptographically secure ("hidden in plain sight") and trustless, eliminating the need for third-party verification. Additionally, while the digital fingerprint is publicly visible, the actual content of the IP remains secure and can function as a trade secret.

The details of the smart contract can remain "invisible" until they are needed to defend the IP in a court of law. Instant IP provides a robust first layer of IP protection, supporting patent law cases involving ownership disputes, origin claims, and proof of prior art. It offers a faster, easier, and more cost-effective solution, saving creators time and money and enabling the proliferation of new ideas.

IP Protection Comparison Chart[IP] (Kary's story)

By now, you've come to learn that I'm a serial entrepreneur. Probably like you, I have multiple ideas every day. And so, as I've mentioned several times throughout the book, I use ALL intellectual property protection tools: copyrights, trademarks, patents, and trade secrets. That said, Instant IP is always the first tool I use because it creates an immutable time stamp. It puts the entire world on notice of when I created the idea.

Another great feature of Instant IP is the ability to hide my idea, essentially also making it a trade secret. It's almost like I "get my foot in the door" and "draw a line in the sand" in terms of when I created my idea. However, I can keep the idea hidden until I need to reveal the details of the smart contract with the simple click of a button.

Also, for clients who come to us with a backlist of unprotected IP from years prior, they can simply put in the description the day they first started using their IP. Although the smart contract is timestamped when they submit their idea via Instant IP, the description can tell the backstory of all the details of first use, and so on.

I'm a visual learner, so when I write books, I often create charts, graphs, and diagrams. (All additional intellectual property, BTW.) By explaining the concept visually, it helps me get a better handle on the concepts. If you find the chart below helpful, reference it within your own IP journey. It's meant to serve as a tool to help you decide which IP you want to protect and how.

IP Protection Comparison Chart [IP]

	Instant IP[TM]	Copyright	Trademark	Patent
Time	1 Minute	2 Months [59]	12-18 Months [60]	1-3 Years [61]
Cost	$97	$500 [62]	$3,000 [63]	$30,000 [64]
Process	1 Click	Forms with Lawyer File with Government	Forms with Lawyer File with Government	Forms with Lawyer File with Government
Protection	Forever	Life of Author Plus 70 Years [65]	5-10 Years [66] (Renewable)	15-20 Years [67]
Benefits	Certificate Instant Timestamp Asset Creation Immutable Secure/Global Public Notice Brand Value Use IP Mark	Certificate Statutory Damages [68]	Public Notice Brand Value Use ® Mark	Exclusive Rights [69] Protection Monetization Opportunities Asset Creation Competitive Advantage
Notes	First/Fast Layer Use the Moment you Create	All Creative Works Start as Unregistered Copyright in the US	Not International "USPTO not an Enforcement Agency" [70]	20 Year Monopoly Fast Track Option Patent Families Real $ Value [71]

Step 7 - Digitize: *Leverage Instant IP as we turn your ideas into digital assets.*

Ready to digitize your IP? We didn't write this book to talk about protecting your IP. Rather, we wanted to give you the tools to start protecting your IP. As a result, we've included a FREE course and a FREE Instant IP Credit for you. To access these benefits, simply scan the QR Code below or visit the URL.

InstantIP.Today/Bonuses

And now for the thinking tool associated with this step. Look at the Instant IP Digitizer[IP]. I've included a blank one as well as a completed version, which I filled out with my own IP and company in mind. Remember, the goal with this step, as well as the other 11, is imperfect action, not perfection.

7. Digitize

Leverage Instant IP™ as we turn your ideas into digital assets.

Component	Concept	Completion
Who	Entrepreneurs who want to increase their influence, impact, and income.[IP]	**Done**
What	Intellectual Property Protection that's faster, easier, and cheaper.[IP]	**Done**
When	The moment you think of an idea is the moment you protect the idea.[IP]	**Done**
Where	Go from Smartphone to Smart Contract[IP]	**Done**
Why	Your Ideas are Valuable. Protect them Today.[IP]	**Done**
How	Create a FREE account at: InstantIP.app	**Done**
1. PRODUCE IP	Don't protect your IP when you're "big." Become "big" by protecting your IP. (Instant IP Harvester[IP])	**Done**
2. PROTECT IP	Use the Instant IP™ Web App on your device. (1) Name it (2) Describe it (3) Protect it	**Done**
3. PROMOTE IP	Leverage: 3 IP Evangelism Essentials[IP] (1) [IP] Superscript (2) QR Code (3) IP Webpage	**Done**
Enterprise	Go Next Level: (1) IP QR Code (2) Hidden/Trade Secret Toggle (3) Value Pricing (4) MFA (5) Transferable Asset Feature	**Done**
Bonuses	Leverage growing IP Toolbox[IP]: Instant IP™ Descriptor [IP], IP Speaker Slide[IP], etc.	**Done**

Instant IP Digitizer[IP]

7. Digitize

Leverage Instant IP™ as we turn your ideas into digital assets.

Component	Concept	Completion
Who	Entrepreneurs who want to increase their influence, impact, and income.[IP]	
What	Intellectual Property Protection that's faster, easier, and cheaper.[IP]	
When	The moment you think of an idea is the moment you protect the idea.[IP]	
Where	Go from Smartphone to Smart Contract[IP]	
Why	Your Ideas are Valuable. Protect them Today.[IP]	
How	Create a FREE account at: InstantIP.app	
1. PRODUCE IP	Don't protect your IP when you're "big." Become "big" by protecting your IP. (Instant IP Harvester[IP])	
2. PROTECT IP	Use the Instant IP™ Web App on your device. (1) Name it (2) Describe it (3) Protect it	
3. PROMOTE IP	Leverage: 3 IP Evangelism Essentials[IP] (1) [IP] Superscript (2) QR Code (3) IP Webpage	
Enterprise	Go Next Level: (1) IP QR Code (2) Hidden/Trade Secret Toggle (3) Value Pricing (4) MFA (5) Transferable Asset Feature	
Bonuses	Leverage growing IP Toolbox[IP]: Instant IP™ Descriptor [IP], IP Speaker Slide[IP], etc.	

Instant IP Digitizer[IP]

This particular thinking tool integrates with the FREE course. I'll walk you through every single step. To start the course, please scan the QR Code above or visit the URL. On that web page, you'll also be able to download a fillable electronic version or print copies for your team.

As always, the sooner you take your IP seriously, the sooner people take you seriously.

IP in Five

1. Digital integration is a necessary strategy to survive and thrive for most businesses, churches, organizations, and universities.

2. "Digitization is a chain reaction of technological progression, a road map of rapid development that always leads to enormous upheaval and opportunity." —Peter Diamandis

3. We feel the untapped potential in data and technological advancements that once seemed far off or impossible are now our reality.

4. What does digitization have to do with intellectual property? Turns out, these days, everything.

5. With a quick upload, an idea can be timestamped, capturing the moment of conception and attributing ownership back to the creator.

8
Monetize:
DETERMINE which IP SOURCES MAKE sense TO YOU.
IP
IP
IP
IP
IP
IP

Disney® Is an IP Company

If you can dream it, you can do it.
—Walt Disney

Ever since his first appearance over a century ago in *Steamboat Willie*, Mickey Mouse has become an iconic figure, an integral part of the second-largest media company in the world. From hand-drawn animation to artificial intelligence, Mickey Mouse represents Disney's persevering brand throughout the ever-changing industry.

Mickey Mouse's creator, Walt Disney, started his career in the entertainment industry, like many before him, by moving to California in 1923. In that place, he and his brother Roy sold his first series, *Alice Comedies*. A few years later, he turned his attention to creating his first fully animated series. Unfortunately, he was cut out of the show by the distributor and discovered he didn't own any rights. From then on, he made it a point to secure the rights for all his future projects.

Little did Disney know his next film, *Steamboat Willie*, would introduce his most recognizable character, Mickey Mouse. Having learned his lesson about intellectual property the hard way, he made sure to secure the rights to Mickey Mouse from day one and went on to create a series of cartoons based on the character. This success spurred on the next milestone, his first feature film, *Snow White and the Seven Dwarves*. Things didn't go as planned, including the amount of money required to produce the film, coming in at 400 percent over budget. Prior to the film, critics came out in droves, calling the film Disney's Folly. He proved them wrong in 1937 when *Snow White and the Seven Dwarves* hit theaters and became one of the highest-grossing films of its time.

Alongside the film's success, a new revenue stream opened up to Disney in the form of merchandising. Other brands approached Disney, seeking to buy the license to use Mickey Mouse's likeness, but Walt wisely maintained full control of his intellectual property.

The studio grew, and it began producing more films in a variety of genres and mediums. Throughout the years, the company adapted to global issues such as World War II, which prompted them to turn their efforts to making two films, *Saludos Amigos* and *The Three Caballeros*, in South America at the request of the state department.

After the war, his studio struggled to find its niche again, eventually creating its first fully live-action film, *Treasure Island*. The masterpiece captured audiences' attention and spurred the production of a slew of other live-action films. Still, Disney saw higher and dreamed bigger. He turned his attention to new expressions of creativity, opening Disneyland® in 1955 in spite of a brand new group of critics. The first theme park of its kind, Disneyland served as an incubator for imagination, regularly adding new attractions and locations.

Now, more than a hundred years later, the Disney brand is still remembered for the animated mouse. Thankfully, Walt Disney took the IP seriously and protected Mickey Mouse, the iconic character. The copyright has been extended multiple times, even becoming the catalyst for the Copyright Term Extension Act of 1998.

Since the expiration of the copyright on January 1, 2024, the original design for Mickey Mouse is now under the public domain. Still, The Walt Disney Company® is known for its due diligence regarding IP protection. Its legal team monitors and manages copyrights and trademarks, keeping much of Mickey Mouse and other characters' likenesses from being used without obtaining licensing.

Walt's initial mistake, signing away his rights to his first animated character, may have helped his company in the long run. Although Disney losing IP rights for his initial creation was a painful lesson, he made securing IP rights for all future inventions a top priority. His tight hold on intellectual property ensures the rights to its films and characters are protected, adding billions of dollars to the bottom line over multiple decades.

Creating an Intellectual Property Holding Company

Since Disney's company is over one hundred years old, its legal structure has changed over the years. That said, several decades ago, it strategically created a separate IP holding company named Disney Enterprises, Inc. One of its functions was copyright holder and trademark owner of Disney-branded intellectual property. The name appears in litigation, court documents, and other venues worldwide to defend the rights of its IP against unauthorized use.[72]

Establishing this type of company is quite common since it provides several benefits. "An IP holding company can be a vehicle to exploit valuable IP while minimizing its exposure to operational liabilities. This separation allows you to protect your IP from both litigants and creditors in the event your operating company is sued."[73] The

IP holding company does not engage in its own day-to-day business activities and serves only as a legal entity for safe-housing intellectual property.

According to Founders Legal:

> An intellectual property holding company is a special purpose business entity, often a corporation or a limited liability company, whose sole purpose is the management and holding of a business's intellectual property assets. The separation of a company's intellectual property assets from its operations serves to protect and shield the intellectual property assets from creditors in the event of litigation or financial insolvency of the operating company.[74]

Simply put, establishing a separate IP holding company could be a smart move, depending on your circumstances. Here are three unique benefits:

1. **Transparency:** The holding company can help attract investors or secure additional funding by providing transparency around the business's revenue-generating assets.[75]
2. **Tax Efficiency:** The holding company may be able to create more efficient tax structures by accruing for IP-related profits in a more favorable tax jurisdiction.[76]
3. **Monetization**: The holding company can license the IP back to the operating company, which produces goods or services.

Of course, there's a right time to consider creating an IP holding company. Here are two times when it makes sense:

1. **Business Groups:** When a business group has multiple connected but distinct entities that share managerial control and use the same IP, the holding company can act as a single entity to safeguard and license the IP to each entity.[77]

2. **Multiple Businesses:** The structure can be useful if a business has multiple businesses that share assets.[78]

Although an IP holding company might be a new concept to some, its validity is time-tested and growing in popularity. According to Aeroleads:

> Some of the notable intellectual property companies in the United States include firms such as IBM, Microsoft, Apple, Google, and Amazon, among others. These companies have a significant impact on the US economy, as they contribute to innovation and job creation in various industries.[79]

If you're new to the topic of an IP holding company, it can feel a bit overwhelming. Taking some time to weigh the pros and cons is often a wise move. On the positive side, there can be tax benefits, especially for global companies. On the negative side, establishing an IP holding company for a corporation raising capital will turn off some investors. They're often hesitant to invest in a company that doesn't own its intellectual property. It's important to consider short-term versus long-term business goals. For example, if a company wants to exit, but also retain its intellectual property, moving assets to a holding company makes sense. Doing so removes the assets from the sale. All in all, consulting with an IP attorney and tax expert is often the next best step when making these important decisions.

Cashing In On Your IP

As we discussed at the beginning of this book, the precise monetary value of IP can be difficult to ascertain without getting a formal valuation completed. However, in the past few years, new data has emerged illustrating the various ways IP can be positioned to extract the maximum return on investment (ROI) for businesses at different stages of growth.

1. **Startup Stage**: For startups trying to attract venture capital, those businesses seeking patents raise more capital than their non-patent-seeking peers. From 2011 to 2020, 58 percent of venture capital went to startups with patents or with patent applications.[80] This fact alone should influence the way start-ups position pitch decks and conversations with angel investors and VC firms.

2. **Growth Stage**: The value-add of IP doesn't stop at funding opportunities. As businesses grow and scale, deal sizes are also positively impacted by IP. Between 2011 and 2020, deal sizes for patent start-ups were 40 percent to 60 percent larger than those for non-patent startups in a given year.[81] And for companies across any stage of growth, patent companies raise capital at significantly higher valuations than non-patent companies.[82]

3. **Exit Stage**: When gearing up for exit or when contemplating potential merger and acquisition strategies, IP can also be positioned for maximum value extraction. Patent-seeking companies exit via the public markets at a rate more than five times higher than non-patent-seeking companies (23.2% versus 4.0%).[83] For acquisition exits, the median exit value for patent companies is 154.9% higher than it is for non-patent companies per year on average.[84]

In conclusion, the value-add of IP is significant. When starting, growing, or exiting a business, you'll come out ahead by taking a proactive and strategic approach to protecting your company's IP. Your future self will thank you as protected IP increases the monetary value of your company in the marketplace.

Step 8 - Monetize: *Determine which IP income sources make sense to you.*

Ready to expand your thinking by discovering 47 ways to monetize your IP? Look at the Instant IP Monetizer[IP]. I've included a blank one as well as a completed version, which I filled out with my own IP and company in mind.

8. Monetize

Determine which IP income sources make sense to you.

Softcover	x	Seminar	x	Spin-Offs	x	Training	x
Hardcover	x	Webinar	x	White Paper	x	Workshop	x
eBook	x	Mastermind	x	Product	x	Roundtable	x
Audiobook	x	Conference	x	Service	x	Investors	
Course	x	Affiliate	x	White Label	x	Lawsuits	
Coaching	x	Partnership	x	Joint Venture	x	Collateral	
Certification	x	Collaboration	x	Experiences	x	Royalties	x
Keynote	x	Subscription	x	Access	x	Securitization	
Content Marketing	x	Podcast	x	License	x	Donation (Tax Strategy)	
Launch Team	x	Vlog	x	Franchise		Capital	
Membership	x	Blog	x	Sale		Shares	
Consulting	x	Article	x	Exit		TEDx	x

Instant IP Monetizer[IP]

8. Monetize

Determine which IP income sources make sense to you.

Softcover	☐	Seminar	☐	Spin-Offs	☐	Training	☐
Hardcover	☐	Webinar	☐	White Paper	☐	Workshop	☐
eBook	☐	Mastermind	☐	Product	☐	Roundtable	☐
Audiobook	☐	Conference	☐	Service	☐	Investors	☐
Course	☐	Affiliate	☐	White Label	☐	Lawsuits	☐
Coaching	☐	Partnership	☐	Joint Venture	☐	Collateral	☐
Certification	☐	Collaboration	☐	Experiences	☐	Royalties	☐
Keynote	☐	Subscription	☐	Access	☐	Securitization	☐
Content Marketing	☐	Podcast	☐	License	☐	Donation (Tax Strategy)	☐
Launch Team	☐	Vlog	☐	Franchise	☐	Capital	☐
Membership	☐	Blog	☐	Sale	☐	Shares	☐
Consulting	☐	Article	☐	Exit	☐		☐

Instant IP MonetizerIP

Getting paid multiple times and multiple ways for creating a single IP asset is a smart and strategic way to increase your influence, impact, and income. In the past 20 years, I've turned my books and my client's books into 18 streams of income. Many of these same 18 income streams show up on the Instant IP Monetizer[IP]. We've also included 29 additional ways IP can be monetized. We're sure you can think of a few more too.

Remember, the goal with this step, as well as the other 11, is imperfect action, not perfection. If you want a short coaching video from me on how to complete the IP exercise, please scan the QR Code below or visit the URL. On that web page, you'll also be able to download a fillable electronic version or print copies for your team.

As always, the sooner you take your IP seriously, the sooner people take you seriously.

InstantIP.Today/Bonuses

IP in Five

1. Although Walt Disney's loss of IP rights for his initial creation was a painful lesson, he made securing IP rights for all future inventions a top priority.

2. An IP holding company can be a vehicle to exploit valuable IP while minimizing its exposure to operational liabilities.

3. While IP holding companies might be a new concept to some, the concept is time-tested and growing in popularity.

4. When starting, growing, or exiting a business, you'll come out ahead by taking a proactive and strategic approach to protecting your company's IP.

5. Getting paid multiple times and multiple ways for creating a single IP asset is a smart and strategic way to increase your influence, impact, and income.

9 Maximize:
IDENTIFY POTENTIAL *Competitors,* CLIENTS & COLLABORATORS.

LEGO® Is an IP Company

Only the best is good enough.
—Ole Kirk Kristiansen, LEGO® Group founder

Billions of LEGO bricks are made every year, each designed with the same stud and tube design since 1958. Few people in America can remember their childhood without these iconic building bricks. However, despite the nostalgic childhood memories they represent, LEGOs were actually born in an era of uncertainty and devastation.

Although the LEGO brick was patented in 1958, the story begins even before 1932 when Ole Kirk Kristiansen founded the LEGO group from two Danish words, "leg godt," meaning "play well."

According to Erin Blakemore, who was writing for the History® Channel, Kristiansen started producing furniture like ladders, stools, and ironing boards.

> In 1924, just as he was looking to expand his successful business, his sons accidentally set a pile of wood chips in the shop on fire.

The flames it produced destroyed the entire building—and the family's home.

Others might have given up with a total loss, but Kristiansen saw the fire as an excuse to simply build a larger workshop. Tragedy continued to strike, however. In 1929, the American stock market crash plunged the world into depression, and Kristiansen's wife died in 1932. Bowed by personal and financial disaster, Kristiansen laid off much of his staff and struggled to make ends meet. Little did he know that those tragedies would lay the foundation for one of business's great comeback stories.[85]

Suffering from the external World War across Europe and from the internal war of personal hardship (his factory burning down once again), Kristiansen made the hard decision to create inexpensive goods that might actually sell. Among them were cheap toys. This, coupled with the lack of resources caused by the war, encouraged Christiansen to look toward alternative materials, namely plastic.

He originally created hollow bricks that could stack together but determined that they lacked the clutch power necessary to build different kinds of structures. So he experimented with several designs and ultimately decided on the stud and tube design that has cemented itself into the LEGO brand. After creating the design, the company knew it needed to patent it in order to keep ideas from competitors and did so on January 28, 1958.[86]

As the bricks continued to sell and the company grew, a new idea formed: the LEGO system in play. The idea was that if all the bricks could fit together in multiple ways, then there was no end to what children could imagine and build with them. The bricks would never lose their value, and there would always be an incentive to buy more bricks with the knowledge they could be used with the old bricks to create entirely new designs.

LEGO continued to thrive and develop their LEGO systems in play, but soon, a new problem arose: the expiring patents that kept competitors from copying the stud and tube bricks. In the absence of a patent, LEGO turned to trademarking as a possibility. When declared "ineligible for trademark protection," LEGO pursued other ways of preserving its market.

As stated in an article by Dennemeyer Group titled, "Everyday IP: The building blocks of LEGO law," the LEGO company:

> Sought to capitalize on earlier achievements by introducing new products compatible with all prior versions—a goal that eventually led to additional releases, including the now-iconic LEGO Minifigure. Launched in 1978, the figure was an improvement over the original LEGO building figure in that it had movable legs that could connect to standard bricks in standing and sitting positions.[87]

LEGO eventually received design rights and used a variety of different measures to protect its intellectual property, including copyright, trademark, design, and trade secrets. Ensuring the quality and uniqueness of its product remains intact, LEGO has fiercely fought for and defended its IP.

I Learned the Hard Way (Kary's story)

By this point in the book, hopefully, you've realized IP is a game you can't opt out of, no matter what story you tell yourself. I've met entrepreneurs who've thought they were "above IP." Others claimed ignorance or busyness as an excuse for ignoring this important topic.

In one recent workshop, I met an entrepreneur who confessed he didn't care if competitors used his unprotected intellectual property. His father's company invented an innovative technology others were starting to copy. "Let them use it," he told us. His carefree attitude sounded generous, but finally, a savvy female entrepreneur called his bluff. "I understand you want to be generous," she said firmly. "Tell me though, if your competitors take your unprotected IP and protect it before you do, locking you out from the very technology you created, then what happens?"

Nobody moved or breathed for that matter.

We turned and stared at the entrepreneur, the one who didn't care about protecting his IP. He swallowed hard and then continued.

"You're asking if my competitor locked me out of my own technology?" he clarified, chuckling nervously. "Well, if that happened, then my father's business...the one I've been charged to run...would be forced to shut down in six months or less," he admitted.

With that honest confession, everyone in the group realized an important truth. We can't abdicate our responsibility for protecting our IP. Whatever excuse we toss out—ignorance, complexity, busyness, or generosity—none holds any weight.

I learned the hard way a few months ago in the form of a cease and desist letter from a very large overseas multi-billion dollar company. (I cannot name the company or the trademark they opposed due to legal issues. Nonetheless, here's the quick story.)

A while back, I named our blockchain solution _____ IP. I went through all the right steps. We did a trademark search. We invested time and money in hiring a law firm to file the correct paperwork. Finally, after more than twelve months, the USPTO granted us the trademark, pending a 30-day oppositional period in which anyone could contest the mark.

Two days before the oppositional period ended, I received an unexpected email from my lawyer.

> *I wanted to bring to your attention that a 30-day Extension of Time to Oppose the "_____ IP" mark was filed. It would be a good idea to have a call to discuss what this means and possible next steps. Do you have any availability tomorrow?*

I wanted to vomit. This is an email you never want to receive. Over breakfast, I told my wife, "I think I'm going to get sued."

We were about two months away from finishing this book. I named the book title: ____ *IP* and registered the ISBNs. It was already listed on Amazon, primed for presales. I just bought a shipment of shirts and jackets for our team bearing the _____ IP logo. We secured the domain name _____ IP and built the corresponding website. We purchased a large _____ IP booth to display at several conferences that booked me to speak and demo the new _____ IP app.

Needless to say, I felt devastated. I couldn't sleep that night. I got up and brainstormed new book names, landing on: *You Are an IP Company.*

Then, I went back to bed, tossing and turning, wondering how I missed our competitor's trademark. Even the USPTO missed it. I'd never heard of this international company. No one had! They didn't even offer the same solution as us.

Still, I couldn't argue with the facts. They had won the timing game, filing _____ IP back in 2004. IP is based on timing. Remember? Timing Is Top[IP]. I knew that more than most. After all, I was the one writing the book on IP and timing—literally. I said those exact words in my TEDx talk viewed by over a million people! That night, I felt dumb—really dumb. Shame and blame flooded my thoughts in nonstop waves.

The next day, my lawyer told me my three options:

1. I could fight them and try to demonstrate the uniqueness of our mark.
2. I could pay some type of licensing fee for the rest of my life.
3. I could rebrand with a new trademark.

It took me about 10 seconds to decide.

Rebrand!

I talked with a few trusted relationships, and we chose the new name Instant IP. I soon loved it even more than the original name. It captured the unique benefit of our app, protecting ideas instantly via the blockchain. It matched my vision of integrating the meaning of abracadabra—I create as I speak—with the world of intellectual property via Instant IP—I protect as I imagine[IP].

Done deal. I have an awesome team. We went to work quickly.

New website.
New shirts.
New app.
New DBA filing with the state of Ohio.

I protected the new brand with our blockchain-based app.[88]
(Kind of ironic, protecting *the new term*: Instant IP with *the new technology:* Instant IP.)

We also filed a new trademark in eight different classes.[89]

All in all, the entire rebrand cost me more than $10,000. I was frustrated for a few days. Then, I shifted my attitude. Many times, it's the only thing we can control—our attitudes. So, rather than anger, I chose gratitude.

I thanked God for getting the lawyer's letter months before the book's release date rather than months after. Rather than dwelling on the typical questions—*Why me?* or *Why now?*—instead, I leaned deep into the question: *What does this make possible?*

And then I wrote a press release based on all the new possibilities, announcing the rebrand, but in a positive light:

_____ IP Rebrands to Instant IP Thanks to Rapid International Growth and Enhanced Capabilities

COLUMBUS, Ohio - Aug. 5, 2024 -- _____ IP™, a leading provider of innovative Intellectual Property solutions, announces a rebrand to Instant IP. This change reflects the commitment to serve its growing international customer base and a new breakthrough for delivering faster, even more efficient services, embodying the capability of its new name: "Instant IP."

Founded in 2021, _____ IP began with a mission for making intellectual property more accessible to individuals and enterprises by reducing the time and cost of protecting unique ideas. Over the past 12 months, _____ IP has experienced increasing global adoption of its patented blockchain-based, smart contract technology.

Now viewed over a million times, Founder Kary Oberbrunner's November 2023 TEDx talk titled Blockchain: The Future of Intellectual Property Protection resonated with those who need a first and fast layer for protecting their ideas. Oberbrunner said, "We need it because ideas now emerge at a dizzying pace. Technology is increasing at an exponential rate thanks to the internet, globalization, and artificial intelligence. Moore's Law reveals technology doubles every 18 months. And knowledge is exploding. It used to double every thousand years, but IBM says it's now every 12 hours. This reality has ushered in a new period called the Creator Economy."

As a result, IP protection is more important than ever. According to the U.S. Patent and Trademark Office, the worldwide sales of counterfeit and pirated goods totals between $1.7 and $4.5 trillion annually. "Sadly, this crime happens every day," explained Oberbrunner. "We all become victims because stealing intellectual property discourages people from creating new ideas. We're not suggesting we need to abolish traditional ways of protecting IP like patents, trademarks, copyrights, and trade secrets. These options might always exist. However, if we want creativity to flourish, we must reduce friction and lower the bar. Thanks to Instant IP, the moment an idea is imagined, it can simultaneously be protected."

Oberbrunner presented the new technology, which is accessible on tablets, computers, and mobile devices, at gatherings in key countries, most notably via a keynote at the London Blockchain Conference in May 2024. His talk, "The Future of Intellectual Property: Leveraging Blockchain to Protect Your Most Valuable Assets Faster, Cheaper, Easier," generated significant interest from global leaders across multiple industries.

Instant IP leverages blockchain technology: a public, digital ledger that provides a distributed record everyone can see but nobody can edit. Oberbrunner said, "Blockchain lowers the bar of intellectual property protection so we can all create. The result is a new renaissance of ideas unleashed in every industry—ideas that make our lives easier and improve our planet."

The rebranding to Instant IP is effective immediately, and the company will be updating its app, website, and communications to reflect the new brand identity. Clients can expect the same level of excellence and innovation that they have come to trust from _____ IP.

The rebrand also includes a new book, *You Are an IP Company*, which releases in Fall 2024. Wall Street Journal and USA Today bestselling author Kary Oberbrunner and Katherine Rubino, a Partner at Caldwell, the fastest-growing law firm in America for more than four years in a row, team up to offer a proven guide for identifying your ideas and protecting them the fastest, easiest, and most effective way possible.

For more information, visit: InstantIP.today

Massive Transformative Purpose

Why share my story of "IP pain" in this book?

For starters, it's because IP protection is real and true and, at times, even messy. Welcome to the creative process. Anyone who tells you otherwise is lying. But take heart, it's also glorious and life-giving and beautiful.

I also shared my story because I wanted to give you hope and encouragement. Intellectual property protection is not always a clear path. It's full of ups and downs. This is why I find it so fascinating. I'm an entrepreneur. I'm in the game. I'm creating new ideas every day, and I'm also learning new insights and nuances every day that help me better understand the journey of intellectual property.

I've realized every expression of IP needs to be defended, whether you protect it with copyrights, trademarks, patents, trade secrets, or Instant IP. Each IP protection tool has unique characteristics and benefits.

This entire conversation surrounding IP captures my attention and my passion. I love helping creatives and companies feel confident about their IP. After all, I've had my IP stolen. Obviously, it's not fun, and when that occurs, our confidence is shattered, and then we stop creating. And when we stop creating, the world suffers.

This is why I rewrote our company's Massive Transformative Purpose.[90]

Our Massive Transformative Purpose

We are the world's only Transformational Publisher that helps abundant-minded and coachable-competent entrepreneurs PUBLISH, PROTECT, and PROMOTE their intellectual property and turn it into 18 streams of income so they can change the world.[IP]

The IP Certification Mark[IP]

Recently, my friend and collaborator Chad Jenkins gave me a great idea. (Chad is the CEO of SEEDSPARK, which I featured earlier in the book.) He told me I needed to give my clients some kind of distinguishing mark they could use when they protected their ideas via Instant IP. I liked his idea. I knew it would give our clients confidence. The mark would tell the world their IP was protected using our blockchain-based solution validated by a unique time-stamped smart contract.

Although I liked his idea, I didn't do anything with it the first four times he told me about it. If you're a fellow creator like me, you know that sometimes it takes a while for us to slow down long enough to let genius advice sink in. Finally, I saw the light and the distinguishing mark. I wondered if I could create something like a ™ except with a superscript [IP] signifying the respective IP expression was backed with a smart contract. I emailed Nick Holmes about the idea, one of my lawyer contacts over at Caldwell. He told me he'd need a little time to research the potential of a certification mark. He said it sounded similar to the concept of an Idaho Potato Certification Mark issued by The Idaho Potato Commission. I thanked Nick with an email reply and, then, looked up more about potatoes in the meantime. Here's what I found:

> Established in 1937, the Idaho Potato Commission (IPC) is a state agency that is responsible for promoting and protecting the famous "Grown in Idaho®" seal, a federally registered trademark that assures consumers they are purchasing genuine, top-quality Idaho® potatoes. Idaho's ideal growing conditions, including rich, volcanic soil, climate, and irrigation, differentiate Idaho potatoes from potatoes grown in other states.[91]

After a couple of days, Nick called me back. I could feel the energy in his voice. I couldn't help but reciprocate his energy since I've come to appreciate and geek out on all things IP. He explained how I could file for a Certification Mark for the superscript [IP] with the USPTO.[92] That's exactly what we did, along with protecting the superscript [IP] via Instant IP.[93]

We named the new IP: The Instant IP Certification Mark[IP]. Now, whenever people use Instant IP to protect their IP, they're immediately granted a forever license to use the superscript [IP] in conjunction with their expression of IP. They're also immediately issued this statement on their official certificate:

> Congratulations. Your IP is now protected. As a result, you have the exclusive right to display the Official The Instant IP Certification Mark [IP] whenever using your respective expression of IP. This Certification Mark usage is granted to the creator indefinitely; however, only for each unique IP expression, which is protected via Instant IP™. For more information, please reference the official statement below.
>
> The superscript symbol [IP] listed is known as the unique certification mark, created and owned by Instant IP™. Its use signifies that the corresponding expression (words, phrases, chart, graph,

etc.) has been protected by Instant IP™ via smart contract. Instant IP™ is designed with the patented smart contract solution (US Patent: 11,928,748), which creates an immutable time-stamped first layer and fast layer identifying the moment in time an idea is filed on the blockchain. This solution can be used in defending intellectual property protection. Infringing upon the respective intellectual property, i.e., [IP], is subject to and punishable in a court of law.

Besides giving our clients confidence, The Instant IP Certification Mark[IP] does something else. It also puts the world on notice that you take your ideas seriously. As a result, they take you seriously. It demonstrates that you are proactive about protecting your intellectual capital and serves to deter potential infringers.

Perhaps a crude example, but ask any thief who's ever "cased the joint"—an idiom meaning to examine a place with the intention of stealing from it later.[94] If thieves believe it's too much effort to trespass and steal property, they simply move on to the next property. Fences, security systems, guard dogs, alarms, and cameras deter them from committing a crime.

The same is true in the world of intellectual property protection. Copyrights, trademarks, and patents, tradesecrets, along with Instant IP and the superscript [IP], tell your competitors to back off. They act as a "fence" around your intellectual property, deterring any would-be infringer from "trespassing." These offensive and defensive IP protection "weapons" discourage thieves from committing an IP crime against you and your company.

Step 9 - Maximize: *Identify potential IP competitors, clients, and collaborators.*

In this chapter, we mentioned competitors, clients, and collaborators. It's important to keep all three on your radar. "'Keep your friends close and your enemies closer' is a phrase attributed to the Chinese military strategist Sun Tzu. The phrase is meant to serve as a reminder to keep an eye on enemies so that their subtle actions can be noticed before they betray or attack."[95]

Look at the Instant IP Maximizer[IP]. I've included a blank one as well as a completed version, which I filled out with my own IP and company in mind.

9. Maximize

Identify potential IP competitors, clients, and collaborators.

Competitors	Clients	Collaborators
IPwe Closed Doors	**Boomer CPA** Knowledge Network	**SEEDSPARK** Business Partnerships
Niftmint Retail	**Emily Raff** Recording Artist	**Caldwell IP** Legal
peerdweb Management	**Dr. Joy Kong** Trade Secret	**USPTO** IP Services
WIPO PROOF Discontinued	**Steve Distante** Author & Thought Leader	**Cedarville** Entrepreneurship
Mintangible NFT Art	**Run Glubz** Running Gear	**Igniting Souls** Publishing Protection

Insights	Instant IP ™ holds a unique position with no competitors because we protected our IP.
Actions	Continue to grow with right fit clients and collaborators. Collaboration is a new competition-free capability.

Instant IP Maximizer^{IP}

9. Maximize

Identify potential IP competitors, clients, and collaborators.

Competitors	Clients	Collaborators

Insights	
Actions	

Instant IP Maximizer[IP]

I intentionally keep certain individuals and organizations at the top of my list. Here's why:

1. **Competitors:** Identifying my competitors helps me maintain my differentiation in the marketplace. Long ago, I decided I'd never compete on price. This is a losing strategy. Instead, I stay focused on providing unique value that no one else can offer.

2. **Clients:** I never want to take any client for granted. That said, certain ones must stay top of mind for certain reasons. Perhaps they're in a situation personally or professionally where they need more time, love, or attention. This thinking tool helps me highlight them.

3. **Collaborators**: I keep my eyes open for massive opportunities. Creating a bigger future means creating right-fit collaborations. By staying self-aware, we attract other self-aware collaborators and explore the potential of creating unique capabilities no one else can offer.

Remember, the goal with this step, as well as the other 11, is imperfect action, not perfection. If you want a short coaching video from me on how to complete the IP exercise, please scan the QR Code below or visit the URL. On that web page, you'll also be able to download a fillable electronic version or print copies for your team.

As always, the sooner you take your IP seriously, the sooner people take you seriously.

InstantIP.Today/Bonuses

IP in Five

1. We can't abdicate our responsibility for protecting our IP. Whatever excuse we toss out—ignorance, complexity, busyness, or generosity—none holds any weight.

2. Every expression of IP needs to be defended, whether you protect it with copyrights, trademarks, patents, or Instant IP. Each IP protection tool has unique characteristics and benefits.

3. When we stop creating, the world suffers.

4. Besides giving our clients confidence, The Instant IP Certification Mark does something else. It also puts the world on notice that you take your ideas seriously.

5. Copyrights, trademarks, and patents, along with Instant IP and the superscript ^{IP}, tell your competitors to back off. They act as a "fence" around your intellectual property, deterring any would-be infringer from "trespassing."

10 Evangelize: CREATE YOUR COMMUNICATION AND Marketing PLAN

Dr Pepper® Is an IP Company

Charles Alderton, a young pharmacist working at Morrison's store, is believed to be the inventor of the now-famous drink. He kept a journal, and after numerous experiments, he finally hit upon a mixture of fruit syrups that he liked. It's now the oldest of the major brand soft drinks in America.
—Dr Pepper Museum

In 1885, Charles Alderton, a chemist who dabbled in making beverages in his free time, created a delicious carbonated soda. He began selling the soda to the customers of the drug store, and it eventually was dubbed Dr Pepper. He had no plans of selling it on a large scale, so he passed it along to Robert S. Lazenby and the store owner, Wade Morrison. They created a bottling company that eventually became Dr Pepper Company.

A turning point in the soda's history was when it debuted at the 1904 World's Fair in St. Louis to the 20 million people in attendance. It caught on quickly, and the mysterious 23-flavor soda soon reached popularity across the country. People were captivated by the strange mix of flavors that tasted distinct but also familiar. To this day, the recipe is kept a trade secret, leaving people to wonder about the 23 flavors.

This mystery, along with the brand's ability to adapt to changing times, has allowed it to remain not only one of the largest soda companies in the world but also the oldest. Throughout the years, the slogans have changed to match the times, going from "King of Beverages," "Old Doc," the "10, 2, and 4" ad campaign, "Be a Pepper," to their most recent slogan, "There's just more to it." Yet, despite their dynamic branding, the recipe and taste remain as timeless as ever.

The Dr Pepper company has grown even larger over the years, expanding to different sodas and drinks. In 2008, the Dr Pepper Snapple Group formed with over fifty soft drinks. Today, it's a unit of the conglomerate Keurig Dr Pepper, which sells coffee and other beverages alongside their soft drinks. According to its website, "Keurig Dr Pepper has a portfolio of more than 125 owned, licensed, and partner brands, leading the way in a wide range of refreshing beverages."[96]

Dr Pepper's secrecy around their unique flavors, which allegedly includes keeping the recipe in two halves in two separate safes at two different banks, has paid off. Despite the proliferation of sodas, Dr Pepper's IP allows it to stand out against competitors time and time again. On June 5, 2024, NPR announced the news: "For the first time, Dr Pepper has surpassed Pepsi® as the nation's No. 2 soft drink. Coca-Cola® is still in first place."[97] Now, over a century later, it's the second highest-selling carbonated soft drink in the United States, proving that millions are still fascinated by the one-of-a-kind taste.

Your IP Is Your Legacy[IP]

Several years ago, my family took a trip to Texas. Although the Dr Pepper Museum wasn't on our list, once we drove by the unique building, we knew we had to stop. "The Museum is housed in the 1906 Artesian Manufacturing and Bottling Company building located in downtown Waco. The 100-year-old building is listed in the National Register of Historic Places as the 'Home of Dr Pepper.'"[98]

The tour was exceptional, and the "Making a Soda" and "Tasting a Soda" experiences proved unique and flavorful. We walked through three levels, observing some of the three hundred thousand Dr Pepper artifacts spread across two large buildings.[99] We saw billboards, articles, ads, and news clippings from the past. Celebrities from decades ago held their Dr Pepper bottles with the slogan "Be A Pepper" splashed across the pages.

Looking back through an IP lens, I now realize the truth. My family and the millions of other visitors who have visited the "museum" in Waco, Texas, since 1991, actually paid for a ticket to tour Dr Pepper's Intellectual Property. It's the legacy of a one-hundred-year-plus IP journey of the carbonated beverage.

Today, Keurig Dr Pepper is the world's 395th most valuable company. Way back in 1885, when Charles Alderton, the young pharmacist, experimented with fruit syrups, he had no idea his beverage would create a worldwide craze, much less an intellectual property company valued at a market cap of $49.64 billion.[100]

Evangelism Essentials and Patent Marking

Sometimes, people want to keep their IP a secret. Historically, this is known as a trade secret.

When designing Instant IP, we wanted to offer this "trade secret" option. As a result, your IP can be hidden or visible depending on your desire. This option is also adjustable inside the app with the press of a button. It allows the contents to remain hidden without the need to disclose them unless you want. We created this toggle capability because we know your IP needs might shift over time. It's the only factor that can be "adjusted" since blockchain technology and smart contracts are immutable.

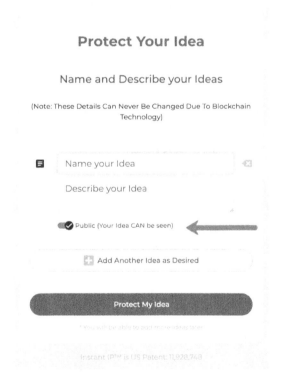

Protect Your Idea

Name and Describe your Ideas

(Note: These Details Can Never Be Changed Due To Blockchain Technology)

Name your Idea

Describe your Idea

Public (Your Idea CAN be seen)

Add Another Idea as Desired

Protect My Idea

Instant IP™ is US Patent: 11,928,748

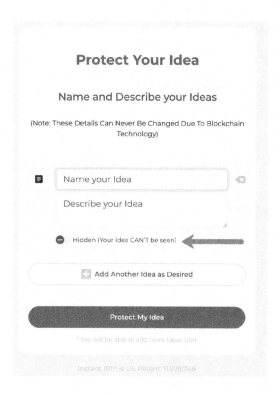

Although the view can be adjusted, the IP can't. In fact, if anyone on the planet (including the creator) tries to change even one part of the protected IP, then the "digital fingerprint" in the smart contract no longer matches. This reveals that the IP has been altered and that it is inauthentic. This factor alerts the world of a bad actor and functions as the ultimate security system for your IP.

In the world of intellectual property, most of the time, you don't want to keep your IP hidden. Rather, you'll want to tell others about IP, including your competitors, clients, and collaborators. Doing so puts "the world on notice" and alerts others about the "fence" around your intellectual property. This is why we named the next phase Step 10-Evangelize. There are many strategies you could implement for "evangelizing" others and putting the world on notice. However, we've narrowed down our favorite, which we've named: The 3 IP Evangelism Essentials[IP].

1. Instant IP Superscript[IP]

This is the cheapest, fastest, easiest way to put the world on notice. It's as easy as 1-2-3.

1. Visit InstantIP.app
2. Enter your IP name and description
3. Press Protect

Your IP is protected instantly via our patented blockchain technology solution. You're also granted the Instant IP Certification Mark, which puts the world on notice that your respective IP is now backed by an immutable, time-stamped, smart contract, proving origin and ownership.

2. Instant IP QR Code

Part of our patented solution includes a corresponding Protected by Instant IP QR Code, which links back to your Protected IP. Rather than just a simple superscript ™ or ®, creators can also include this QR code on their physical products (see below).

In fact, we include it on the back of every book we publish. This way, when consumers scan the QR code, they go straight to the Protected IP vault and view the time-stamped, immutable, smart contract by clicking on the respective Protected IP. Immediately, people know this creator and company take their IP seriously.

3. IP Web Page

We recommend the strategy modeled by our collaborator and client, Suman Kanuganti, Co-Founder and CEO of Personal AI.[101] Suman holds multiple patents for his IP. He created a web page so anyone can find this IP quickly and easily.

- Check it out at: Personal.ai/ip Pretty cool? See where it forwards?

Suman also wanted to leverage Instant IP for his patents by turning them into digital assets with the press of a button. Using our blockchain technology, we turned them into smart contracts.

- Suman's Protected IP page: Instantip.today/protected

I liked Suman's web page strategy so much that I followed his example for my own IP.

- My IP web page: InstantIP.today/IP

Guess who also else uses this strategy? Dr Pepper, of course.[102]

- Dr Pepper IP web page: KeurigDrPepper.com/patents

This web page serves as a resource to inform consumers and competitors about the breadth of protection regarding Keurig Dr Pepper's intellectual property portfolio.

The 3 IP Evangelism Essentials also complements a "patent marking" strategy. If you have patents, then "marking" them is not only a strategic decision but also a financial one too. In an article titled "What is 'Virtual Patent Marking' and Does It Make Sense for Your Business?," author Christopher Proskey explains more:

> Marking your products with your patent numbers informs your customers, and perhaps more importantly, your competitors, that the product is indeed patented. This can have a chilling effect on potential infringers. Marking your products as patented also serves a marketing function and supports the perception of value and innovativeness of the product.[103]

It all comes down to notice and putting the world on notice about your patent portfolio. In the event of a failure to mark a patented article, damages in an infringement action may only be recovered in the time period after the infringer was provided notice of the infringing activity. In some instances, this may be years down the line, meaning significant sums of money are being left on the table by the patent owner if they fail to integrate patent marking with their IP.

Step 10 - Evangelize: *Create your IP communication and marketing plan.*

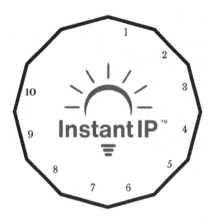

As we've encouraged throughout the book, make sure you protect your IP before you promote your IP. Do this by implementing the 3 IP Evangelism Essentials. Then, you can put the world on notice through the Instant IP Evangelizer[IP]. I've included a blank one as well as a completed version, which I filled out with my own IP and company in mind.

10. Evangelize
Create your IP communication and marketing plan.

Purpose	Platform	Post
Rebrand	Press Release	Instant IP™ Rebrands Thanks to Rapid International Growth and Enhanced Capabilities
Value Creation	Forbes	The Costs Of IP Theft And How To Protect Your Company's Ideas
Credibility	TEDx	Blockchain: The Future of Intellectual Property Protection
Awareness	Forbes	Steps For Safeguarding Your Intellectual Property In The Digital Era
Thought Leader	Spotify	You are an IP Company Podcast with Katie Rubino
Authority	Everywhere	Co-Authored Book: Print, eBook, Audiobook
Value Creation	Forbes	37 Strategies To Monetize Your Intellectual Property And Earn More Influence, Income And Impact
Credibility	Audible	Podcast: The Intellectual Capitalist with Tony D'Angelo

Insights	Now that my IP is protected it's time to promote it.
Actions	Implement a PR strategy using Igniting Souls as my marketing team.

Instant IP EvangelizerIP

10. Evangelize

Create your IP communication and marketing plan.

Purpose	Platform	Post

Insights	
Actions	

Instant IP Evangelizer^{IP}

Notice the 3Ps: Purpose, Platform, and Post. Make sure to follow this order within your evangelism efforts:

1. **Purpose:** Identify your purpose by attaching meaning to your message.
2. **Platform:** Choose the platform you want to use.
3. **Post:** Create a post and then publish it.

Remember, the goal with this step, as well as the other 11, is imperfect action, not perfection. If you want a short coaching video from me on how to complete the IP exercise, please scan the QR Code below or visit the URL. On that web page, you'll also be able to download a fillable electronic version or print copies for your team.

As always, the sooner you take your IP seriously, the sooner people take you seriously.

InstantIP.Today/Bonuses

IP in Five

1. Sometimes, people want to keep their IP a secret. Historically, this is known as a trade secret.

2. Most of the time, you'll want to tell others about IP, including your competitors, clients, and collaborators. Doing so puts "the world on notice" and alerts others about the "fence" around your intellectual property.

3. There are many strategies you could implement for "Evangelizing" others and putting the world on notice. We've narrowed down our top 3, which we've named: 3 IP Evangelism Essentials.

4. The 3 IP Evangelism Essentials[IP] complements a "patent marking" strategy.

5. Notice the 3Ps found within the Instant IP Evangelizer[IP]: Purpose, Platform, Post. Make sure to follow this order within your evangelism efforts.

11 Globalize: DEVELOP A GROWTH STRATEGY to EXPAND IP impact

Apple® Is an IP Company

Your time is limited, so don't waste it living someone else's life.
Don't be trapped by dogma, which is living with the results of
other people's thinking.
—Steve Jobs

Although many ideas start in garages, only one has become the most valuable company in the world.[104] Back in 1976, two college dropouts, Steve Jobs and Steve Wozniak, had a dream of creating user-friendly computers. After building the Apple I and finding moderate success, they turned their attention to the Apple II, a model that revolutionized computers through its colored graphics. At a time when computers were just beginning to become mainstream, Apple® set itself apart for being a step ahead and anticipating the desire for more usable home and personal computers.

Year after year, Apple improved the original computer many times over. But it didn't just stop at computers. In 2007, it released the iPhone. The design combined the functionality of a cell phone with the user-friendly design of the iPod®. The device revolutionized cell phones and quickly became mainstream, with each subsequent iPhone building on the previous to make it easier to use and more functional. Although other companies created their own devices similar to the iPhone, Apple trademarked the term and functions, forcing others to find their own names and designs for their handheld devices.

Apple created many other successful products, including the iPad®, AirPods®, Apple Watch®, and more. It dominates the tech industry, winning over the masses year after year because of the quality and ease of its products. Apple's user-friendly interface gives the average person confidence when using technology products.

Apple protects its IP with patents ranging from the home button to screen displays. Its branding transcends logos and includes the shape of devices like rounded edges. Some customers even save Apple packaging materials, impressed with the look and feel. Apple's consumer unboxing videos often go viral, proving it cracked the code of making IP an experience. This globalized company is a fan favorite across the world.

Going Global with IP Strategy

Today, we live in a global economy. Goods, services, and assets move between countries at record speed thanks to the internet, connected devices, AI, and many other types of technology. As a result, every company is now both an IP company AND a global company. Wise companies recognize this and proactively develop and implement a global IP strategy.

Protecting IP in one country allows you to protect and enforce your IP in that jurisdiction, but it does little to stop competitors abroad. When we look at successful brands like Chanel®, Facebook®, Amazon®, Microsoft®, and PayPal®, they have at least one thing in common: intentionally establishing global brand recognition. A school child in Norway recognizes an Apple® computer just as much as an office worker in San Francisco. This truth builds value and notoriety for these companies.

When strategizing about your own global protection, it's important to ask yourself a few questions.

1. What are the largest markets for my goods or services?
2. Where might my product be manufactured?
3. Are there specific markets I aim to enter down the road?

Once you've answered these questions, you can start creating a plan. Different countries have different laws surrounding IP enforcement, and factoring these into your answers will help clarify other areas where you'll need additional IP protection.

In the United States, the patent system allows for complex damages. This means patent infringers are liable for monetary awards. In other countries, this isn't always the case, and enforcement might only result in injunctions. While this may stop the infringing behavior, it does little to provide retribution. Working with a skilled IP professional can assist companies in creating global strategies that balance these competing demands.

Patent Families Create More Value

Katie Rubino, my brilliant co-author, has incredible insight and experience when it comes to the strategy of creating patent families. After I received my first patent for Instant IP, she asked if I wanted to create a patent family. Part of me saw only the price tag—more time and more money—but the other part of me saw her wisdom. I knew I wanted to go big on Instant IP. I saw firsthand how we provided a real solution for entrepreneurs around the world. I also knew the need for establishing more "creative space" so we could keep on expanding and improving the blockchain-based technology and help more creators and companies protect their IP faster, cheaper, and easier.

Looking back, I'm so glad we took Katie's advice. We filed a child patent immediately, and since then, we've already created several amendments to reflect breakthroughs in our Instant IP app.

Here's why it's such a powerful strategy. When a first patent application is allowed, this "parent application" has the ability to be kept open by filing a "child application," also known as a continuation application. The continuation application relates back to the filing date of the parent application but has patent claims (the legally enforceable part of the patent) focused on a different invention. For this reason, parent patent applications tend to be drafted quite robustly to strategically create downstream monetization opportunities through continuation applications.

The rationale for continuation applications is multi-faceted, creating additional value for the inventor in three main ways:

1. **Protection:** Continuation applications allow us to reinforce our fence of protection more strongly. Weak fences get knocked down easily. With more layers, our fence strengthens, and with more claims around different inventions, the stronger our patent protection becomes.

2. **Priority:** We've said it many times before in this book: IP protection comes down to timing (Timing Is Top[IP]). Continuation applications date back to the filing date of the parent application. As time passes, this becomes more important and significant, allowing us to file new continuations that claim priority to a filing date several years prior. As new competitors enter the scene, the patent holder will be able to get ahead of these market entrants and create new opportunities for monetization.

3. **Profit:** Continuation applications increase the monetary value of a patent portfolio. If you stop the patenting process after your parent patent application is approved, the value of your asset is roughly $229,000. (See part 1 for more information.) However, by continuing the process and creating a patent family via filing a continuation application, the asset value increases to $325,000.

Step 11 - Globalize: *Develop a growth strategy to expand your IP impact.*

What's your growth strategy?
How big do you want to get?
Who do you want to impact?

Maybe you already know the answers to these questions. Or maybe this is the first time you've ever considered them.

Look at the Instant IP Globalizer^{IP}. I've included a blank one as well as a completed version, which I filled out with my own IP and company in mind.

11. Globalize

Develop a growth strategy to expand your IP impact.

IP Impact	Coach abundant-minded entrepreneurs on IP protection.
IP Action	Start the Instant IP Optimizer[IP]. A select coaching community.
IP Outcome	Transformational IP education, networking, and collaboration.

IP Impact	Make IP a mainstream topic accessible to right fit audience.
IP Action	Start You Are an IP Company Podcast with Katie Rubino.
IP Outcome	Listeners gain courage by seeing themselves in case studies.

IP Impact	Equip next gen entrepreneurs with IP tools and tactics.
IP Action	Integrate IP in role as Chair of Entrepreneurship at Cedarville.
IP Outcome	Students gain IP clarity and competence in their businesses.

IP Impact	Igniting Souls authors leverage books as IP income streams.
IP Action	Offer Instant IP™ and IP harvest as standard in all proposals.
IP Outcome	Our authors are differentiated as global IP industry leaders.

Instant IP Globalizer[IP]

11. Globalize

Develop a growth strategy to expand your IP impact.

IP Impact	
IP Action	
IP Outcome	

IP Impact	
IP Action	
IP Outcome	

IP Impact	
IP Action	
IP Outcome	

IP Impact	
IP Action	
IP Outcome	

Instant IP Globalizer[IP]

For me, this is a powerful thinking tool. Whenever I complete it, I find myself discovering another way to expand my IP impact. This time, I realized Katie and I should create a new podcast. And so we did. Perhaps you'll be a future guest. We want to highlight creators and companies who implement the 12 Steps.

On that topic, we want to encourage you to keep going. You're on Step 11 and almost at the finish line. Remember, the goal with this step, as well as the other 11, is imperfect action, not perfection. If you want a short coaching video from me on how I complete the IP exercise, please scan the QR Code below or visit the URL. On that web page, you'll also be able to download a fillable electronic version or print copies for your team.

As always, the sooner you take your IP seriously, the sooner people take you seriously.

InstantIP.Today/Bonuses

IP in Five

1. Sometimes, people want to keep their IP a secret. Historically, this is known as a trade secret.

2. Most of the time, you'll want to tell others about IP, including your competitors, clients, and collaborators. Doing so puts "the world on notice" and alerts others about the "fence" around your intellectual property.

3. There are many strategies you could implement for "Evangelizing" others and putting the world on notice. We've narrowed down our top 3, which we've named: 3 IP Evangelism Essentials.

4. The 3 IP Evangelism Essentials[IP] complements a "patent marking" strategy.

5. Notice the 3Ps found within the Instant IP Evangelizer[IP]: Purpose, Platform, Post. Make sure to follow this order within your evangelism efforts.

12 Optimize: Enjoy IP FREEDOM, FINANCES ✓ & FULFILLMENT!

Magnolia® Is an IP Company

It's up to us to choose contentment and thankfulness
now—and to stop imagining that we have to have
everything perfect before we'll be happy.
—Joanna Gaines, *The Magnolia Story*

Waco, Texas, has been home to many since its establishment in 1849. For one couple, it was not only a place to call home but an opportunity to flip houses into homes for others.

Chip and Joanna Gaines are possibly best known for their hit TV series, *Fixer Upper*, a reality show that ran for five seasons on HGTV, where the couple helped people buy and renovate homes in Waco. Since then, they and their Magnolia Farms® brand have expanded into all the facets of a home. Fans of Magnolia can shop in their stores, eat in their restaurants and bakery, read their magazines, use their cookbooks, and even watch their favorite shows via the Magnolia TV network.

One way they've grown their company while keeping the brand consistent and unique is through their trademarks. Magnolia Business Ventures LLC has fifty-one different trademarks on specific goods and events. They've trademarked some of their slogans for apparel, such as "#DEMODAY"[105] and "#shiplap."[106] They strategically structured their corporate arm, so their IP Holding Company (Magnolia IP Holdings LLC) owns some of their intangible assets.

With so many different aspects to their company and the wide range of goods and services, on the surface, it might seem difficult to stay under one brand. However, Magnolia has remained unified, and the payoff is undeniable. The Gaines have built an IP engine, evidenced by marketing savviness and steadily growing customer loyalty and trust. It works because all of the Magnolia sub-brands focus on the home in some way.

Although the Gaines isn't a perfect family, nor is Magnolia a perfect company, both are great examples of how protected IP creates more freedom, finances, and fulfillment.

Freedom: A Place to Keep Creating

IP protection makes space to keep innovating. Remember my TEDx mentioned at the beginning of the book? I highlighted the research study done by the American Society of Landscape Architects, which asked teachers to take their preschool classes to two different playgrounds in a nearby busy city.[107] If you recall, the playgrounds were exactly the same, except one playground had no fence, and the other was surrounded by a fence.

In the first scenario, the children huddled around their teacher. They didn't explore or play. Rather, they stayed by her side, afraid to venture out. But the second playground produced different results. Here, the same children played on all the equipment and freely explored all the way up to the edge of the fence.

This isn't simply a cute story about preschool kids on playgrounds. Rather, it's a commentary on creators and companies. Without fences, we're not free to create and collaborate.

Although patents can be thought of as monopolies, with clear structures in place, they can be leveraged to advance technology. As the saying goes, "Good fences make good neighbors." And for willing parties who grant permission, good fences also allow neighbors "to play on each other's properties" as we continue creating and innovating.

Finances: IP Options for Every Business

IP protection gives access to new financing opportunities. My friend Steve Distante, author of *Pitchology*, recently interviewed Alex LePage, founder of MillerHill IP, a prominent intellectual property consulting and valuation firm. In their chat, LePage shares the power of intellectual property to secure capital without giving up equity. This is extremely relevant to early-stage businesses that don't have significant revenue but who have an asset—the technology they have protected. While these assets, like patents and trademarks, have been termed "intangible," MillerHill IP has developed a rigorous strategic process to quantify the qualities that make them unique and thus valuable.

> Many startups may only have an idea; some might have a small amount of revenue with an Alpha or Beta product. But one thing is true in nearly every case: startups and growth-stage companies alike need capital to get to the next stage of growth, to fund production, hire, and go to market. We provide due diligence and proprietary analysis to facilitate the loan process. As you might expect, part of this includes the due diligence around the size of the market, differentiation of the product, and the sales and

marketing strategy. However, of equal importance is the quality and comparative characteristics of the patent portfolio. By providing a rigorous analysis related to the specific economic opportunity tied to the IP, we can often help founders obtain a loan, which avoids giving away equity. This favorable outcome is often measured in tens to hundreds of millions of dollars in value that the startup preserves.

Their fascinating interview goes into depth on how to position your intellectual property to obtain funding and set yourself up for more freedom, finances, and fulfillment. Retaining equity in your company is only one example.[108]

Fulfillment: Patent Pledges Increase Collaboration

IP protection opens new doors for greater fulfillment. Often, when we think of IP, we imagine a David and Goliath scenario. Some companies own large quantities of IP (Goliaths), and other smaller companies own a few intangible assets, if any (Davids). These two companies often function as competitors who battle out IP rights and royalties to the death.

Thankfully, it doesn't have to be this way. IP collaboration can advance technology and aid in humanitarian efforts.

Look no further than Elon Musk. In June 2014, he announced Tesla's patent pledge, allowing anybody acting in good faith to use Tesla's patents. Musk's rationale was simple and noble. Tesla couldn't solve the electric car problem alone, and instead, the company sought collaboration.

What Tesla did was noteworthy for a few reasons. First, Tesla strategically set up a pool of assets that it recognized as being instrumental to advancing electric vehicles. As the ultimate beneficial owner of these patents, Tesla has the ability to control how others utilize these patents. Second, for the identified patents, they set up an open-source structure whereby, to this day, anybody who wants to be able to use these patents to advance the development of electric vehicles is able to do so. Tesla recognized the monumental nature of the problem they wanted to solve. The greater the contribution and innovation from multiple parties, the more quickly a solution could be brought to market.

IP collaboration isn't restricted to just automobiles. We've also seen the power of patent collaboration in other areas. During various health crises, drug manufacturers waived patent infringement liability for governments and suppliers to produce medications at scale to treat outbreaks of common diseases. As a result, life-saving solutions aided those most in need.

When considering a collaboration, it's important to have an agreement in place to identify IP ownership. Typically, these agreements acknowledge each party in the collaboration may independently own any IP acquired before the collaboration starts. This is what we call "background" IP, that is, IP owned before any collaboration has begun. In some situations, parties may license their background IP to one another. Any IP created throughout the collaboration is considered "foreground" IP—IP created during the pendency of the collaboration.

It's important that any rights relating to ownership of foreground IP are called out in an IP agreement. You don't want to get down the road in your collaboration and have to sort out after the fact who owns what IP. Obviously, this is uncomfortable and costly to resolve a problem that could have been negotiated at the start. Think of these agreements akin to prenuptial agreements. It's always easier to lay out expectations at the start and prepare for contingency arrangements if something does go wrong, than to try and fix a problem after the start when emotions can be high.

Step 12 - Optimize: *Enjoy your IP freedom, finances, and fulfillment.*

Ready to imagine how IP can give you new levels of freedom, finances, and fulfillment?

As an entrepreneur, I'm incredibly blessed to be on the frontlines, helping entrepreneurs create new IP every day. This is the unique position I have as the CEO of a publishing company. And for the past twenty years, I've seen how my own books—intellectual property—have opened new doors in terms of relationships and opportunities.

"Words create worlds," said theologian Abraham Joshua Heschel. And so, with this final thinking tool—Instant IP Optimizer[IP]—it's time to step into a new world of possibilities.

12. Optimize

Enjoy your IP freedom, finances, and fulfillment.

Freedom	Finances	Fulfillment
I speak on IP protection in new locations meeting new people, always adding value.	Students and new entrepreneurs can get in the game faster and win.	Blockchain utility onboards more people to Web 3.
Ability to protect new ideas the moment I imagine them.	We reduce cost and friction for idea protection.	Instant IP™ exposes more authors to Igniting Souls®.
Ideas spread faster and farther due to IP protection.	New capability creates more collaborations & more impact.	IP protection is now more accessible to all creators.
Authors bring more life change faster due to IP clarity, courage and confidence.	New products and services to entrepreneurs. New markets mean more income.	Integrates well with Entrepreneurship Chair and student biz launches.
IP cause grows organically with IP mark & QR codes.	Patented Instant IP QR codes create retail product wins.	More ignited souls: creators, consumers, collabs.
The SaaS model and new app create huge scalability.	Success grows currency of influence creating more good.	An OPUS match to create synergistic partnerships.
Self Multiplying Company.	Opportunity to give more.	Novelty and Risk = Flow.

Insights	My IP is much bigger than me, creating exponential impact.
Actions	I must act courageously, spread the message, & stay focused.

Instant IP Optimizer IP

12. Optimize

Enjoy your IP freedom, finances, and fulfillment.

Freedom	Finances	Fulfillment

Insights	
Actions	

Instant IP Optimizer^{IP}

Remember, the goal with this step, as well as the other 11, is imperfect action, not perfection. If you want a short coaching video from me on how to complete the IP exercise, please scan the QR Code below or visit the URL. On that web page, you'll also be able to download a fillable electronic version or print copies for your team.

As always, the sooner you take your IP seriously, the sooner people take you seriously.

InstantIP.Today/Bonuses

IP in Five

1. Good fences make good neighbors. Without fences, we're not free to create and collaborate.

2. By providing a comprehensive IP valuation, the founder can obtain loans and avoid being forced to give up equity to VC investors.

3. IP collaboration can advance technology and aid in humanitarian efforts.

4. The greater the contribution and innovation from multiple parties, the more quickly a solution could be brought to market.

5. When considering a collaboration, it's important to have an agreement in place identifying IP ownership.

PART THREE
START

Protect Your IP Today

Congratulations! You've reached the final part of our IP journey together. And yet, for many readers, their IP journey is just beginning. This is why we call Part 3: Start.

In writing this book, one thing is very clear. Most of the companies and creators we've featured in the book had no clue how far they'd go. And yet, each took their IP seriously. This is one of the central themes of the book, referenced back in the Taylor Swift chapter.

You don't protect your IP because you're big. You become big by protecting IP.

Big means different things to different companies. Perhaps you aspire to bigger influence, impact, or income, not matter. Regardless, IP protection isn't something you can ignore. We've said this at the end of each of the 12 steps, and it's worth mentioning one final time:

The sooner you take your IP seriously, the sooner people take you seriously.

Remember Tiffany's and the color it trademarked: Tiffany Blue? This company takes its IP so seriously that, according to its website:

> Tiffany Blue® was eventually adopted for all of Tiffany's packaging and branding. True to the founder's vision, the Tiffany Blue Box® is as much an icon of luxury and exclusivity as it was a century ago. As *The New York Sun* reported in 1906, "[Charles

Lewis] Tiffany has one thing in stock that you cannot buy from him for as much money as you may offer; he will only give it to you. And that is one of his boxes. The rule of the establishment is ironclad, never to allow a box bearing the name of the firm, to be taken out of the building except with an article, which has been sold by them and for which they are responsible." This rule is still enforced today, maintaining the Box's coveted status and honoring Tiffany's vision.[109]

History proves that although you can never start protecting your intellectual property too early, most people start too late. In a game where timing is everything, the time to protect your intellectual property is now.

Since the bar is lowered for protecting intellectual property in terms of the cost of time and money, nobody has an excuse for not taking action. As someone who's benefitted from Caldwell, I highly recommend them for traditional ways of protecting intellectual property. I've been a client for many years, and I rely on them throughout the year for my intellectual property strategy.

And if you need a first layer and a fast layer to protect your intellectual property, may I suggest Instant IP. It may not be your last step, but because of its time-stamping technology, it could always be your first step. As the creator and founder, sure, I'm biased. Then again, I'm the first user, and I rely on it weekly when protecting my own IP. I believe the world benefits from a simple blockchain-based solution to help companies and creators just like you. We need the ability to instantly go from: Smartphone to Smart Contract[IP].

As an entrepreneur who works with amazing entrepreneurs, I know ideas come *to us* and *through us* often when we least expect them. I can't shake the word abracadabra—meaning I create as I speak. I also can't shake Instant IP—meaning I protect ideas as I produce ideas.

Our enemy is friction, and as long as there are multiple layers of friction between our ideas and the ability to protect them, the world will keep being robbed of our creativity. Katie and I believe in a better way and a better world.

It's been an honor for us to serve as your tour guides on this most important topic. By now, we hope you've caught the main mission of our book. Protecting your IP is secondary. First and foremost, this book is an invitation for you to shift your identity.

On that note, we'll start where we began, way back in the beginning. Next time someone asks you who you are and what you do, there's only one correct answer.

I Am an IP Company...

...And I create Intellectual Property.

Appendix:
Intellectual Asset Management (IAM)
Resource List

We are not endorsing these resources, nor are we receiving any financial compensation for listing them. We are merely seeking to be helpful as you navigate your IP journey.

IP Organizations

- **The World Intellectual Property Organization:** (www. wipo.int) A specialized agency of the United Nations. One of WIPO's principal objectives is to promote synchronized laws and practices regarding IP among its member states. Another core task for WIPO is to help protect IP by allowing members to file for international patents and trademarks, as well as by offering arbitration and mediation to individuals and businesses in order to resolve IP disputes. WIPO has a free online database that allows users to search for IP data.

- **The International Trademark Association**: (www.inta.org) A not-for-profit membership association dedicated to the support and advancement of trademarks and related intellectual property as elements of fair and effective commerce. INTA supports its network of 5,700 trademark owners by advocating for effective and harmonized international trademark laws.

INTA's website provides resources for researching trademark law and initiatives.

- **Licensing Executives Society International:** (www.lesi.org) An association of 32 national and regional societies that focuses on the transfer of technology and licensing of intellectual property rights. LESI has more than ten thousand individual members, including representatives of companies, scientists, engineers, academicians, governmental officials, lawyers, patent and trademark attorneys, and consultants. A core LESI objective is to encourage professional standards among individuals engaged in the transfer and licensing of technology and industrial or intellectual property rights. LESI assists members in improving their skills in the licensing trade. LESI sponsors educational meetings and publishes reports and articles relating to licensing.

- **The American Intellectual Property Law Association** (www.aipla.org) A national bar association constituted primarily of lawyers in private and corporate practice, in government service, and in the academic community. AIPLA produces a number of informative publications pertaining to IP law. AIPLA is also actively involved in shaping US intellectual property policy and has started a worldwide campaign to reduce the costs of procurement and enforcement of patents and trademarks.

- **The National Inventor Fraud Center:** (www.inventor-fraud.com) Provides consumers with information about invention promotion and how to market ideas without falling victim to companies that sell the marketing of inventions but do not realize any results for the inventors.

IP Research

- **RefAware:** (www.refaware.com) A web-based service that monitors the internet in order to provide its members with updates of peer-reviewed and non-refereed sources of information shortly after they are posted online. Users can create distinct searches in order to track new developments in their area of interest.

Online Licensing Exchanges

Note: Licensing exchanges serve as electronic marketplaces linking licensors and licensees. Some of the websites also act as licensing agents and consultants, as well as exchanges.

- **Tech Transfer Online:** (www.wipo.int/technology-transfer) Online exchange where users can post and search for IP. The website also facilitates secure sales and licensing of IP.

- **PriorIp:** (priorart.ip.com/index.html) A research tool that uses sophisticated algorithms to cluster innovations and patent applications. This clustering allows the user to find patent information and then easily find related patents.

- **Yet2.com:** (www.yet2.com) Provides an online source where IP owners can post their IP to a searchable database. Yet2.com also provides a marketplace where its members can license and sell IP.

- **Flintbox:** (www.flintbox.com) is a platform for universities, corporations, entrepreneurs, and technology communities to seek out collaborators for their own innovations or find innovations in which they want to participate.

Patent Brokers

Note: These companies can assist in the sale of intellectual assets.

- **Private IP Brokerage from Ocean Tomo®:** (www.oceantomo.com) Practice consists of providing advisory services for intellectual property transactions.
- **Vitek**: (www.vitek-ip.com) Practice consists of buy-side and sell-side patent brokerage services.
- **Mobity**: (www.mobity.com) Practice consists of patent sales and acquisitions.
- **Tangible IP**: (tangibleip.biz) Practice consists of patent brokerage and strategic advisory.

Patent Auctions

- **IPv4 Global**: (www.ipauctions.com) An online marketplace where ownership of IP is auctioned off to the highest bidder.

IP Valuation Firms

Note: These companies can assist in valuing your intellectual assets.

- **MillerHill IP**: (www.millerhillip.com) A leading intellectual property consulting and valuation firm.
- **Richardson Oliver Law Group**: (www.richardsonoliver.com) An intellectual property valuation firm that can assist with buying, selling, and evaluating the price of assets in M&A, bankruptcy, or when looking for an internal transfer price.
- **Foresight Value Smart™**: (www.foresightvaluation.com) An intellectual property (IP) valuation, strategy, and economic consulting firm.

Direct Licensing Firms

Note: These companies will directly acquire or fund your IP and seek to license it and/or enforce it themselves.

- **Acacia Research Corporation:** (Nasdaq: ACTG) (www.acaciaresearch.com/patent-licensing) Engaged in the business of acquiring patent rights for licensing and enforcement. Acacia becomes the owner or exclusive licensee of the patent portfolio and enforces the IP rights, giving its clients a percentage of the recovery.

- **General Patent Corporation:** (www.generalpatent.com) Litigates against corporations that have infringed on IP rights of owners who cannot afford to pursue litigation on their own. General Patent Corporation works on a contingency-fee basis.

R&D Licensing Companies

Note: These companies are focused on highly specific industries and will license your IP from you, conduct R&D, and then incorporate the IP into their own products and technologies, which they then license and sell.

- **MOSAID Technologies, Inc.** (TSE: MSD) (www.mosaid.com) An IP company focused on the licensing and development of semiconductor and communications technologies. Mosaid's core business is the licensing of patented semiconductor and communications IP. A key to Mosaid's strategy is to expand its patent portfolio through licensing partnerships and patent acquisitions.

- **Tessera Technologies, Inc.** (Nasdaq: TSRA) (www.techonline.com/directory/tessera-technologies/) Licenses and delivers innovative miniaturization technologies that transform next-generation electronic devices. Tessera invests in and develops this technology.

Patent and IP Buyers

Note: These companies will purchase your IP directly from you.

- **Intellectual Ventures:** (www.intellectual ventures.com) Uses a business model that centers on creating, acquiring, and licensing inventions in a variety of technology areas. IV commercializes inventions through licensing, spin-offs, joint ventures, and industry partnerships.

- **Allied Security Trust (AST):** (www.ast.com) A Delaware statutory trust that was originally formed by several high-technology companies to obtain cost-effective patent licenses. The Trustees' freedom to sell provides opportunities to enhance company products by sharing the cost of patent licenses. The Trust creates new opportunities for patent holders.

- **RPX Corporation:** (www.rpxcorp.com) Acquires patent rights that could be used against its members in patent enforcement litigation. The RPX Defensive Patent Aggregation does not require member involvement in acquisitions, and RPX will not enforce the patents it purchases.

IP holders who believe their patents are being infringed can get infringement litigation funding from these firms:

- **Curiam Capital**: (www.curiam.com) Provides financing for high-value litigation.
- **Fortress**: (www.fortress.com) Provides investor-oriented alternative investment solutions and resources.
- **Burford Capital**: (www.burfordcapital.com) A financial services company that provides specialized finance to the legal market.

Notes

1   Oberbrunner, Kary. "Blockchain: The Future of Intellectual
    Property Protection." Filmed November 2023 in
    Oshkosh, WI. TEDxOshKosh. https://www.youtube.com/
    watch?v=pA19Tf5wFEA&t=192s

2   U.S. Intellectual Property and Counterfeit Goods—Landscape
    Review of Existing/Emerging Research. February 2020. Accessed
    October 2, 2023. https://www.uspto.gov/sites/default/files/
    documents/USPTO-Counterfeit.pdf.

3   Macro Trends. "S&P 500 Index - 90 Year Historical Chart."
    Accessed October 18, 2024. https://www.macrotrends.net/2324/
    sp-500-historical-chart-data.

4   Johnson, Matthew. "Ocean Tomo Releases Intangible
    Asset Market Value Study Interim Results for 2020."
    Ocean Tomo. September 22, 2020. https://oceantomo.
    com/insights/ocean-tomo-releases-intangible-asset-marke
    t-value-study-interim-results-for-2020.

5   Lin, Vic. "How much does a patent cost from start to finish?"
    PatentTrademarkBlog. https://www.patenttrademarkblog.com/
    how-much-patent-costs.

6   Shafiz, Usman. "Can PQAI Save Inventors from Failing at The
    Patent Office?" PQAI. September 26, 2024. https://projectpq.ai/
    patent-rejection.

7   Yuan, Yuanling and John Constantine. "What is the creator
    economy?" SignalFire.com. November 29, 2020. https://signalfire.
    com/creator-economy.

8   US Patent and Trademark Office. "First Inventor to File (FITF)
    Resources." Accessed October 18, 2024. https://www.uspto.gov/
    patents/first-inventor-file-fitf-resources.

9   In the Know. "Why do some McDonald's only have a single golden arch?" September 9, 2022. https://www.intheknow.com/post/why-do-some-mcdonalds-only-have-a-single-golden-arch.

10   Nevil, Scott. "Distributed Ledger Technology (DLT): Definition and How It Works." Investopedia.com. Updated June 28, 2024. https://www.investopedia.com/terms/d/distributed-ledger-technology-dlt.asp.

11   Bench, Jonathan. Are Smart Contracts Legal Contracts? April 26, 2023. https://harrisbricken.com/blog/are-smart-contracts-legal-contracts.

12   Summerlin, Peter. "ASLA 2006 Student Awards: Magnolia River Ranch." American Society of Landscape Architects. Accessed October 18, 2024. https://www.asla.org/awards/2006/studentawards/282.html.

13   Firmino, Luiz. "Abracadabra: I will create as I speak." LinkedIn. March 2, 2023. https://www.linkedin.com/pulse/abracadabra-i-create-speak-luiz-firmino-cissp-cism-crisc-cciso/.

14   These numbers are based upon 2023. The information is updated on an annual basis.

15   Richardson Oliver Insights. *Patent Market Data Actionable Analytics. ROI 2023 Report.* Published April 10, 2024. https://static1.squarespace.com/static/62e409548ddf9a45093621ec/t/66b10f5a88b9d7360874eb86/1722879838352/It+was+a+Great+Time+to+Buy+Patents+in+2023+-+The+Brokered+Patent+Market+2023+-+IAM+Media+-+20240410.pdf.

16   Bates-Brownsword, Darryl. "Unleashing the Power of Intangible Assets with Andrew Sherman." Exit Insights, episode 92. https://www.youtube.com/watch?v=Ney58UbE5vI.

17   The Drum Team. "1975: Cola wars heat up with launch of Pepsi challenge." March 31, 2016. https://www.thedrum.com/news/2016/06/14/marketing-moment-75-cola-wars-heat-1975-launch-pepsi-challenge.

18   Lubin, Peter S. and Patrick Austermuehle. "John Deere Wins Trademark Case Regarding its Green and Yellow Colors." (blog)

Chicago Business Litigation Lawyer Blog. January 15, 2018. https://www.chicagobusinesslitigationlawyerblog.com/6049.

19 Ibid.

20 Tiffany & Co. Newsroom. https://press.tiffany.com/our-story/ tiffany-blue.

21 Bob Smietana, "Who Owns the Pastor's Sermon?," Christianity Today, January 2014, https://www.christianitytoday.com/2014/01/ who-owns-sermon-church-pastor.

22 The Strategic Coach Team. "Dan Sullivan's Best Career Advice: 10 Secrets To Success For Today's Entrepreneur." (blog). Strategic Coach. https://resources.strategiccoach.com/ the-multiplier-mindset-blog/dan-sullivans-best-career-advice-1 0-secrets-to-success-for-todays-entrepreneur.

23 "Life and Career." Taylor Swift Museum. https://www. theswiftmuseum.com/life-and-career.

24 Williamson, Marianne. "Our deepest fear is not that we are inadequate." Marianne Williamson, A Return to Love: Reflections on the Principles of "A Course in Miracles. Goodreads. com. https://www.goodreads.com/quotes/928-our-deepes t-fear-is-not-that-we-are-inadequate-our.

25 Comer, John Mark. *Live No Lies: Recognize and Resist the Three Enemies That Sabotage Your Peace.* Colorado Springs, CO: Waterbrook, 2021.

26 "Krispy Kreme Corporation Records." Smithsonian. Accessed October 21, 2024. https://www.si.edu/object/archives/ sova-nmah-ac-0594.

27 Buonaiuto, Abigail. "The Story of Krispy Kreme." JohnLocke. org. Accessed October 21, 2024. https://www.johnlocke.org/ the-story-of-krispy-kreme.

28 Harris. Tom. "How Krispy Kremes Work." HowStuffWorks.com. https://science.howstuffworks.com/innovation/edible-innovations/ krispy-kreme.htm.https://science.howstuffworks.com/innovation/ edible-innovations/krispy-kreme.htm.

29   "Krispy Kreme Doughnut Corporation." Encyclopedia.com. https://
www.encyclopedia.com/books/politics-and-business-magazines/
krispy-kreme-doughnut-corporation.

30   Buonaiuto. "The Story of Krispy Kreme."

31   "5 Famous Trade Secrets People Use Everyday." Emerson
Thomson Bennett. April 2, 2024. https://www.etblaw.com/
famous-trade-secrets.

32   Crosbie, Eve. "Shark Tank: 7 Biggest Missed Investments
That Went on to Make Millions." HELLO! April 9, 2021.
https://www.hellomagazine.com/film/20210409110706/
shark-tank-biggest-missed-investments.

32   Crosbie, Eve. "Shark Tank: 7 Biggest Missed Investments
That Went on to Make Millions." HELLO! April 9, 2021.
https://www.hellomagazine.com/film/20210409110706/
shark-tank-biggest-missed-investments.

33   Fowle, Harry. "How Much Did Jamie Siminoff Sell Ring For?"
February 13, 2024. ioT Insider. https://www.iotinsider.com/news/
how-much-did-jamie-siminoff-sell-ring-for.

34   Enjoli, Audrey. "Kodiak Cakes: Here's What Happened After
Shark Tank." Food Republic. September 28, 2023. https://www.
foodrepublic.com/1405423/kodiak-cakes-shark-tank-now.

35   "Lindsay Stirling - Trademark Details." Justia Trademarks.
Accessed October 21, 2024. https://trademarks.justia.com/859/83/
lindsey-85983404.html.

36   "Ode to Sleep." Twenty One Pilots (video). Accessed October 21,
2023. https://www.youtube.com/watch?v=2OnO3UXFZdE.

37   "Twenty One Pilots - Trademark Details." Justia Trademarks.
Accessed October 21, 2023. https://trademarks.justia.com/854/69/
twenty-one-85469220.html.

38   Sullivan, Dan. "This Tool Will Help You Make Sense Of The
Past AND Take Charge Of Your Future." (blog). Strategic Coach.
Accessed October 21, 2023. https://resources.strategiccoach.
com/the-multiplier-mindset-blog/this-tool-will-help-you-mak
e-sense-of-the-past-and-take-charge-of-your-future.

39   Sullivan, Dan. "What Is Intellectual Property & How to Protect It."
      (video). Strategic Coach. Accessed October 21, 2023. https://www.
      youtube.com/watch?v=7EeV68t8baA.

40   "Trademark, Patent, or Copyright." US Patent and Trademark
      Office. Accessed October 21, 2023. https://www.uspto.gov/
      trademarks/basics/trademark-patent-copyright.

41   "Trademarks and Trade Dress." Lucas & Mercanti LLP.
      Accessed October 21, 2023. https://www.lmiplaw.com/
      trademarks-and-trade-dress.

42   "Just the Facts: Intellectual Property Cases—Patent, Copyright, and
      Trademark." U.S. Courts. February 13, 2020. https://www.uscourts.
      gov/news/2020/02/13/just-facts-intellectual-property-cases-paten
      t-copyright-and-trademark.

43   "The Complete Set of Simple Tools." EOS Worldwide. Accessed
      October 21, 2023. https://www.wipo.int/wipoproof/en/.

44   "The Complete Set of Simple Tools." EOS Worldwide. Accessed
      October 21, 2023. https://www.eosworldwide.com/eos-tools.

45   "Get a Grip Glossary of EOS Terms." EOS Worldwide. Accessed
      October 21, 2023. https://www.eosworldwide.com/wp-content/
      uploads/2020/12/EOSWW.Get_.A.Grip_.Glossary.pdf.

46   Hormozi, Alex. "I've said it before, give away the secrets." TikTok
      video. April 11, 2023. https://www.tiktok.com/@ahormozi/
      video/7220826611011095854.

47   Legal Information Institute. s.v. "genericide." Accessed October 21,
      2023. https://www.law.cornell.edu/wex/genericide.

48   Legal Information Institute.

49   Yang, Michelle. "How to Avoid the Fate of Brand Genericide."
      LegalVision. Accessed October 21, 2023. https://legalvision.com.
      au/brand-genericide.

50   Genesis 2:19-20,NIV.

51   "FORTNITE - Trademark Details." Justia Trademarks. Accessed
      October 21, 2023. https://trademarks.justia.com/854/88/
      FORTNITE-85488103.html.

52   Cuny, Gaston. "When Did FORTNITE Really Come
      Out? The Exact FORTNITE Release Date." MSN.com.

Accessed October 21, 2023. https://www.msn.com/en-ca/
news/technology/when-did-FORTNITE-come-out-th
e-exact-FORTNITE-release-date/ar-AA1ljNxM.

53 "Redeem your V-Bucks Card." FORTNITE. Accessed October 21,
2023. https://www.FORTNITE.com/vbuckscard.

54 "Emotes." FORTNITE WIKI. Accessed October 21, 2023. https://
FORTNITE.fandom.com/wiki/Emotes.

55 Diamandis, Peter. "The 6 Ds." (blog) Diamandis.com. November
21, 2016. https://www.diamandis.com/blog/the-6ds.

56 Peter Diamandis and Steven Kotler, *Bold: How to Go Big, Create
Wealth and Impact the World,* Simon & Schuster, 2015.

57 https://www.visualcapitalist.com/
the-soaring-value-of-intangible-assets-in-the-sp-500

58 Ibid.

59 https://www.copyright.gov/registration/docs/
processing-times-faqs.pdf

60 https://www.uspto.gov/trademarks/basics/
how-long-does-it-take-register

61 https://allendyer.com/how-long-does-it-take-to-get-a-patent

62 https://wellsiplaw.com/how-much-does-a-u-
s-copyright-registration-cost

63 https://counselforcreators.com/log/trademark-cost

64 https://www.superlawyers.com/resources/patents/
how-much-does-a-patent-cost/

65 https://www.copyright.gov/help/faq/faq-duration.html

66 https://www.uspto.gov/learning-and-resources/trademark-faqs

67 https://www.uspto.gov/web/offices/pac/mpep/s2701.html

68 https://www.copyright.gov/help/faq/faq-general.html

69 https://www.nibusinessinfo.co.uk/content/
advantages-and-disadvantages-getting-patent

70 https://www.uspto.gov/trademarks/basics/
why-register-your-trademark

71 https://www.roipatents.com

72 "Terms of Use." The Walt Disney Company Museum. Accessed
October 21, 2024. https://www.waltdisney.org/terms-use.

73 Wilson, John. "Creating an Intellectual Property Holding Company." Wilson Whitaker Rynell. June 19, 2024. https://www.wilsonlegalgroup.com/blogs/business-law/ ip-holding-company-setup.

74 "What Is an Intellectual Property Holding Company?" Founders Legal. Accessed October 21, 2024. https://founderslegal. com/leveraging-intellectual-property-holding-companies-t o-protect-and-exploit-your-ip-assets

75 "5 Ways an IP Holding Company Could Benefit Your Business." Metis Partners. Accessed October 21, 2024. https://metispartners. com/thought-leadership/5-ways-an-ip-holding-company-cou ld-benefit-your-business.

76 Goldner, Esq., Bruce and Mackinzie Neal, Esq. To hold or not to hold: Considerations in creating an IP holding company." Westlaw Today. November 20, 2020. https://www. skadden.com/-/media/files/publications/2020/11/tohoTo hold or not to hold: Considerations in creating anIP holding companyldornottoholdconsiderationsincreatinganipholdi.pdf.

77 "Intellectual Property Holding Company: Why You Need One." (blog). Offshore Protection. Updated September 12, 2023. https://www.offshore-protection.com/offshore-blog/ intellectual-property-holding-company.

78 "3 Benefits Of A Holding Company—And How To Structure Your Businesses." Forbes. November 9, 2023. https://www.forbes.com/ sites/allbusiness/2023/11/09/3-benefits-of-a-holding-company-and-how-to-structure-your-businesses.

79 "Top Intellectual Property Companies In The United States Of America." Aeroleads. Accessed October 21, 2024. https:// aeroleads.com/list/top-intellectual-property-companies-in-unite d-states-of-america.

80 White, Andy and Ulan James. *Introducing PitchBook Patent Research. Takeaways on patents' impact on startup success.* Published February 6, 2023. https://pitchbook.com.

81 Ibid.

82 Ibid.

[83] Ibid.

[84] Ibid.

[85] Blakemore, Erin. "The Disastrous Backstory Behind the Invention of LEGO Bricks." Updated January 30, 2024. https://www.history.com/news/the-disastrous-backstory-behind-the-invention-of-lego-bricks.

[86] "Toy building brick." Google patents. Accessed October 21, 2024. https://patents.google.com/patent/US3005282A/en.

[87] "Everyday IP: The Building Blocks of LEGO Law." Dennemeyer. January 29, 2024. https://www.dennemeyer.com/ip-blog/news/everyday-ip-the-building-blocks-of-lego-law.

[88] "Transaction Details - Instant IP." Polygonscan. Accessed October 21, 2024. https://polygonscan.com/tx/0xb80800b76a8d3fefa15c191e3de63a8fa1a73e1facf7b3455e0d4d497afbad9a.

[89] "Trademark Status & Document Retrieval (TSDR) - Instant IP Trademark." US Patent and Trademark Office. Accessed October 21, 2024. https://tsdr.uspto.gov/#caseNumber=98675910&caseSearchType=US_APPLICATION&caseType=DEFAULT&searchType=statusSearch.

[90] Thanks for teaching me the MTP concept, Peter Diamandis and Salim Ismail. https://web.openexo.com/exo-model/massive-transformative-purpose.

[91] "Certification Marks." Idaho Potato Commission. Accessed October 21, 2024. https://idahopotato.com/licensing/certification-marks.

[92] "Trademark Status & Document Retrieval (TSDR) - IP Certification Mark." US Patent and Trademark Office. Accessed October 21, 2024. https://tsdr.uspto.gov/#caseNumber=98697863&caseSearchType=US_APPLICATION&caseType=DEFAULT&searchType=statusSearch.

[93] "Transaction Details - Instant IP." Polygonscan. Accessed October 21, 2024. https://polygonscan.com/tx/0xb80800b76a8d3fefa15c191e3de63a8fa1a73e1facf7b3455e0d4d497afbad9a.

[94] *Cambridge Dictionary Online.* s.v. "case the joint (phrase). https://dictionary.cambridge.org/us/dictionary/english/case-the-joint.

95 Dennis, Raymond. "Keep Your Friends Close and Your Enemies Closer? Not In Cyberspace." November 2019. https://www.usni.org/magazines/proceedings/2019/november/keep-your-friends-close-and-your-enemies-closer-not-in-cyberspace.

96 "Our Brands." Keurig Dr Pepper. Accessed October 21, 2024. https://keurigdrpepper.com/brands.

97 "Dr Pepper surpasses Pepsi — is the 2nd-most-popular carbonated beverage in the U.S." NPR.org. June 5, 2024. https://www.npr.org/2024/06/05/nx-s1-4993527/dr-pepper-surpasses-pepsi-is-the-2nd-most-popular-carbonated-beverage-in-the-u-s.

98 "History of Dr Pepper Museum." https://drpeppermuseum.com/history/history-of-dr-pepper-museum.

99 "Dr Pepper Museum." City of Waco Convention and Visitors. Accessed October 21, 2024. https://destinationwaco.org/places/dr-pepper-museum-main.

100 "Keurig Dr Pepper (KDP)." Companies Market Cap. Accessed October 21, 2024. https://companiesmarketcap.com/keurig-dr-pepper/marketcap.

101 While on topic, I recommend Personal AI. I'm also a client and his team created my own AI, which helps me simultaneously save time and create value.

102 "Patents." Keurig Dr Pepper. Accessed October 21, 2024. https://keurigdrpepper.com/patents.

103 Proskey, Christopher. "What is 'Virtual Patent Marking' and Does It Make Sense for Your Business?" March 28, 2023. https://www.brownwinick.com/insights/what-is-virtual-patent-marking-and-does-virtual-patent-marking-make-sense-for-your-business.

104 https://www.visualcapitalist.com/ranked-the-50-most-valuable-companies-in-the-world-in-2024

105 "#DEMODAY - Trademark Details." Justia Trademarks. Accessed October 21, 2024. https://trademarks.justia.com/870/46/demoday-87046559.html.

106 "#SHIPLAP - Trademark Details." Justia Trademarks. Accessed October 21, 2024. https://trademarks.justia.com/869/82/shiplap-86982620.html.

[107] Summerlin, Peter. "Magnolia River Ranch." American Society of Landscape Architects 2006 Student Awards. https://www.asla.org/awards/2006/studentawards/282.html.

[108] "Leveraging IP to Raise Capital with Alex LePage." The Entrepreneurland Podcast, Ep. 8, https://www.youtube.com/watch?v=gkRVn569NJQ.

[109] "Tiffany Blue." Tiffany & Co. Accessed October 21, 2024. https://press.tiffany.com/our-story/tiffany-blue.

Acknowledgments

Kary Oberbrunner thanks:

To the world changers at our companies, Igniting Souls and Instant IP. I'm blessed to work alongside you. Thanks for *letting me* stay in my lane and *making me* stay in my lane. Sarah Grandstaff, Jamie Chambers, Tanisha Williams, Melissa Fultz, Ruthie Bult, Travis Leonard, Travis White, Jill Ellis, Lori Piotrowski, Sheila Davis, Elizabeth Haller, Lynne Modranski, Micaela Eberly, and Teri Kojetin.

To the experts at Teammate AI. Your incredible skills helped us bring our IP vision to life via the Instant IP app. Evan Ryan, Bill James, Kristian Tanninen, Maciej Krupowies, and Jason Cisarello.

To Keegan Caldwell, Katherine Rubino, Nick Holmes, and everyone at Caldwell IP. You understood our vision and then protected our vision. We would not be where we are without your partnership and professionalism.

To Strategic Coach®, and specifically Dan Sullivan and Babs Smith, for opening my mind to a brand new world called Intellectual Property. Thanks for connecting us with the key Whos to help us achieve our How. I am deeply indebted.

To Cedarville University, and specifically Dr. Thomas White, Dr. Thomas Mach, and Dr. Jeffrey Haymond. Your belief and support for me staying in the game as an entrepreneur allows me to bring my best to the incredible students and classrooms on this beautiful campus.

To my family: Kelly, Keegan, Isabel, and Addison. Thanks for letting me explore my "peculiar" passions, in this case, intellectual property protection. I love creating memories with you.

Katie Rubino thanks:

To our team at Caldwell for their relentless dedication, passion, and enthusiasm. Your daily contributions fuel our shared mission, and together, we achieve great things…Kegan Caldwell, Micah Drayton, and Marcus Wolter.

To Kary Oberbrunner, Sarah Grandstaff, Ruthie Bult, and all our friends at Instant IP and Igniting Souls. Thank you for your friendship and shared vision for this project. It is an honor to be a member of your community.

To Dan Sullivan and Babs Smith at Strategic Coach®, thank you for your mentorship and introduction to Freezone®. I feel lucky that our paths crossed, and I appreciate your continued insights and support.

To my clients, thank you for your inspiration, vision, and trust. Your belief in me drives me to keep going.

To the entrepreneur community, thank you for your creativity and pursuit to bring new technology to market. Keep innovating and moving the goalpost forward.

To my friends and family, thank you for your continued encouragement and for being my number one supporter.

About the Authors

Kary Oberbrunner

Dr. Kary Oberbrunner is a *Wall Street Journal* and *USA Today* best-selling author of 14 books. As CEO of Igniting Souls and Instant IP, he helps abundant-minded & coachable-competent entrepreneurs PUBLISH, PROTECT, and PROMOTE their intellectual property and turn it into 18 streams of income so they can change the world.

An award-winning novelist, screenwriter, and inventor, he's been featured in *Entrepreneur*, *Forbes*, CBS, Fox News, Yahoo, and many other major media outlets. His TEDx has been viewed over 1 million times.

As a young man, he suffered from severe stuttering, depression, and self-injury. Today a transformed man, Kary ignites souls: speaking internationally on a variety of topics and consulting the world's top entrepreneurs and brands regarding publishing, protecting, and promoting intellectual property.

He has several earned degrees, including a Bachelor of Arts, a Masters in Divinity, and a Doctorate in Transformational Leadership.

He also serves as the Berry Chair of Entrepreneurship at Cedarville University, where he teaches on the topics of entrepreneurship and digital marketing. Kary enjoys cycling, especially in the French Alps. He lives in Ohio with his wife Kelly and three children: Keegan, Isabel, and Addison.

Katherine Rubino

Katie is a partner and director of Caldwell's life science practice group. Katie focuses on the representation of life sciences companies discovering, developing, protecting, and offering pharmaceuticals, therapeutic vaccines, digital health, medical devices, biologics, and antibody products.

Katie has been featured in *The Wall Street Journal*, Fox Business, and *Nature Biotechnology* for her intellectual prowess in governing legal and scientific disputes. Katie specializes in transactions involving intellectual property rights, strategic partnerships, licensing, and research collaborations. In addition, she maintains an active practice in cross-border transactions, being dually qualified to practice in the United States, England, and Wales.

Katie is the past chair of the Chemistry and the Law division of the American Chemical Society. She is a fixture of the entrepreneurial ecosystem and provides pro-bono legal advice in partnership with MIT Sandbox and Oregon Bioscience Incubator.

About Igniting Souls

Igniting Souls is the world's first and only Transformational Publisher that helps abundant-minded and coachable-competent entrepreneurs PUBLISH, PROTECT, and PROMOTE their intellectual property and turn it into 18 streams of income so they can change the world. If that's you and if you need help, then start the conversation today: IgnitingSouls.com/Apply.

About Caldwell

Innovation is in our DNA

1. Monetization

A return on investment is essential. We excel at helping clients devise and execute programs to optimize the value of their companies. Our team counsels on all aspects of the monetization process, from harvesting and mining to identifying valuable assets, evaluating the market for those assets, and generating revenue.

2. Team First

We act as primary legal counsel for over 50 of our client companies. We integrate with our clients to understand their industry, assets, and liabilities, and we have their back when the going gets tough.

3. Transparent Trust

We believe that trust is a core principle upon which every relationship must be grounded. Our guiding values are to be open, honest, and straightforward. We are not afraid to reject the status quo and, instead, strive to continue to grow in our ability to deliver authentic truths. We integrate with our clients to form a cohesive team that is focused on a shared vision. We believe in each other, and we believe in serving as a true partner who can help accomplish any mission.

4. Empirical Strategy

There is a winner and a loser. We know how to win. No smoke in the mirror. Just facts and laser-focused strategy on getting the win every time we open a matter for our clients.

YOUR IDEAS ARE VALUABLE

Instant IP™

PROTECT THEM TODAY

InstantIP.Today

THIS BOOK IS PROTECTED INTELLECTUAL PROPERTY

Instant IP™

The author of this book values Intellectual Property. The book you just read is protected by Instant IP™, a proprietary process, which integrates blockchain technology giving Intellectual Property "Global Protection." By creating a "Time-Stamped" smart contract that can never be tampered with or changed, we establish "First Use" that tracks back to the author.

Instant IP™ functions much like a Pre-Patent™ since it provides an immutable "First Use" of the Intellectual Property. This is achieved through our proprietary process of leveraging blockchain technology and smart contracts. As a result, proving "First Use" is simple through a global and verifiable smart contract. By protecting intellectual property with blockchain technology and smart contracts, we establish a "First to File" event.

Protected by Instant IP™

LEARN MORE AT INSTANTIP.TODAY

Made in the USA
Monee, IL
13 November 2024

70041002R00134